DATE DUE

JUN 23 1979			
FEB 25 1980			
Renewed to man 10-1980			
MAR 30 1981	HWS 5/17/10		
OCT 2 1981			
JUN 29 1982			
JAN 17 1984			
DEC 1 1984			
SEP 18 1987			
MAR 17 1989			
28 1992			
AUG 22 1994			
JAN 12 1996			
FEB 6 1998			
OCT 20 1999			
HWS 5/17/10			

GAYLORD   PRINTED IN U.S.A.

D0919618

THE PUBLIC LIFE OF SHERLOCK HOLMES

The
Public Life
of
Sherlock Holmes

Catalogued and described by
MICHAEL POINTER

DRAKE PUBLISHERS INC.

For
ANTHONY HOWLETT
*who once impersonated Sherlock
Holmes in Switzerland, but
that's another story*

Published in 1975 by
Drake Publishers Inc.
381 Park Avenue South
New York, New York 10016

ISBN 0-87749-725-7
LCCCN 74-12785

Printed in Great Britain

Contents

List of Illustrations

Acknowledgements

This book grew out of my friendship with Anthony Howlett, which began while we were at school together, when he prepared what must have been the first list of Sherlock Holmes dramatisations, based on Vincent Starrett's *The Private Life of Sherlock Holmes* and our own cuttings. My special thanks to him for all our joint research.

Much of the information in this book is published for the first time, and is based on personal interviews, discussions and correspondence over many years with actors, directors, writers, historians, collectors and enthusiasts. I am particularly grateful to Sir Felix Aylmer, Ted Bergman, Peter Blau, Clive Brook, Jacques Deslandes, Ronald de Waal, Denis Gifford, Cornelis Helling, A. D. Henriksen, Jack Howarth, Kay Hutchings, Stanley Mackenzie, Raymond Mander and Joe Mitchenson, Nicole Milinaire (the Duchess of Bedford), Bjarne Nielsen, the late Eille Norwood, Albert Parker, the late George Pearson, Raymond Raikes, Peter Sallis, Ray Selfe, Anthony Slide, Harry Towb, Alan Wheatley and the late Arthur Wontner.

I must also thank the librarian and staff of Grantham Public Library, the staff of the British Film Institute Information and Cataloguing Departments, and the staff of the British Museum Newspaper Library for years of helpful service. Thanks, too, to the editors of *The Sherlock Holmes Journal* and the RSC bulletin *Flourish* for permission to adapt pieces originally written for them.

Quotations from Sir Arthur Conan Doyle's Sherlock Holmes Long and Short Stories are by kind permission of John Murray (Publishers) Ltd/Jonathan Cape Ltd and Baskervilles Investments Ltd. The quotation from *The Vagrant Mood* is by permission of The Estate of

W. Somerset Maugham and William Heinemann Ltd. Stills are copyright of the companies named in the captions.

Finally, I am indebted to Mary and Martin Pointer for their help in preparing this book for publication, and to Adelaide Griffin for kindly typing it all.

The Man in the Mind's Eye

Dr. Conan Doyle's remarkable detective, Sherlock Holmes,
has achieved the distinction of stage treatment – which is, after
all, a somewhat common fate of remarkable characters.

Glasgow Herald (1894)

Among the many well-known characters of the world's fiction there
are a few whose names will never be forgotten. Because of their fame
and popularity these great characters frequently appear in dramatisations in which they are impersonated by well-meaning actors, directed
by well-meaning directors or produced by well-meaning producers.

But the results of their good intentions seldom meet with our un-
qualified approval, for as we have read the works of fiction concerned,
our imagination has developed an image in the mind's eye, and attempts
by others to reproduce that character often disappoint us.

Nevertheless, audiences have derived immense pleasure from the
many dramatisations of their fictional favourites that have been presented on the stage, the cinema screen and more recently the television
screen.

Certain of these works are adapted and repeated over and over again,
but their attraction and popularity never seem to wane. The works of
Charles Dickens are prominent in this category, both for stage and
screen, as are those of Alexandre Dumas, Robert Louis Stevenson,
H. G. Wells, Somerset Maugham, Edgar Rice Burroughs, Zane Grey
and countless others.

But the character whose dramatised adventures far exceed those of
any other fictional individual is Sir Arthur Conan Doyle's unique
creation – the consulting detective Sherlock Holmes. Conan Doyle

must be one of the world's most adapted authors, for many of his other literary works have provided rich sources for dramatists and script writers, but it is the Sherlock Holmes stories that have proved to be so lastingly popular, and that have been used, copied, altered, and generally plundered for the purposes of entertainment.

Such is the durability of Sherlock Holmes that any account of his dramatised adventures tends to form a miniature history of public entertainment over the last eighty years: stage plays, revue sketches, silent films, sound films, comedy films, radio plays, television plays, gramophone records, a musical and even a ballet. (So far we have been spared the spectacle of Sherlock Holmes on ice!)

Ask anyone to describe Sherlock Holmes and they are almost certain to mention a deerstalker hat, a curved pipe and the expression, 'Elementary, my dear Watson'. As a matter of fact, none of these appears in any of the Conan Doyle stories, but thanks to the artists who have illustrated the stories, and the writers and actors who have dramatised Sherlock Holmes, these things have become part of the generally accepted image of Sherlock Holmes.

If one adds to this accepted convention the characteristics that *are* recorded by Conan Doyle (the astonishing powers of observation and deduction, the remarkable knowledge of unusual subjects, the violin playing, all the various idiosyncrasies), there emerges a figure that the world of entertainment has embraced with warm affection. Somerset Maugham wrote of Sherlock Holmes:

> He was drawn in broad and telling lines, a melodramatic figure, with marked idiosyncrasies which Conan Doyle hammered into the minds of his readers with the same pertinacity as the great advertisers used to proclaim the merits of their soap, beer or cigarettes, and the results were as remunerative. You know no more of Sherlock Holmes after you have read fifty stories than you did after reading one, but the constant reiteration has broken down your resistance; and this lay figure decked out with theatrical properties, has acquired the same sort of life in your imagination as is held by Vautrin or Mr. Micawber. No detective stories have had the popularity of Conan Doyle's and because of the invention of Sherlock Holmes I think it may be admitted that none has so well deserved it.

In the course of a conversation in the story *The Valley of Fear* Sherlock Holmes is particularly revealing about the theatrical side of his nature:

Watson insists that I am the dramatist in real life. Some touch of the artist wells up within me and calls insistently for a well-staged performance. Surely our profession . . . would be a drab and sordid one if we did not set the scene so as to glorify our results. The blunt accusation, the brutal tap on the shoulder – what can one make of such a *dénouement*? But the quick inference, the subtle trap, the clever forecast of coming events, the triumphant vindication of bold theories – are these not the pride and the justification of our life's work? At the present moment you thrill with the glamour of the situation and the anticipation of the banter. Where would be that thrill if I had been as definite as a timetable?

Literary arguments have raged, and no doubt will continue, over the degree to which Conan Doyle and subsequent authors have been indebted to Edgar Allan Poe and his three Auguste Dupin short stories, which preceded the first Sherlock Holmes story by over fifty years. Dupin, with his remarkable intellect, simply sat at home with his unnamed friend and reasoned out the solutions to certain criminological problems. But regardless of how much Doyle may have been influenced by these stories, there can be no denying that it was Sherlock Holmes and Dr Watson who set the pattern for consulting detectives and their assistants for decades to come, and they have achieved a popularity that would never have been possible for Poe's rather bloodless and immobile characters.

Unlike Dupin, Sherlock Holmes is a combination of intellect and action, and the actions arising from his intellectual exercises have to be explained to the willing but less perspicacious Dr Watson. This is an attractive arrangement for both readers and audiences, for we don't mind being a few steps behind Sherlock Holmes in understanding what is going on, so long as we can be just a few steps ahead of Dr Watson.

Innumerable detective-story writers have followed this idea and given their brilliant sleuths a down-to-earth aide to whom it all has to be spelt out – Dr Thorndyke and Dr Jervis, Hercules Poirot and Hastings, Inspector Hanaud and Ricardo, Nero Wolfe and Archie Goodwin; the list is endless but none of them approach the eminence accorded to Sherlock Holmes and Dr Watson.

In one of the last of the stories, Dr Watson finally arrives at a full realisation of *his* purpose in the partnership:

The relations between us in those latter days were somewhat peculiar. He was a man of habits, narrow and concentrated habits, and I had become one of them. As an institution I was like the violin, the shag tobacco, the old black pipe, the index books, and others perhaps less excusable. When it was a case of active work and a comrade was needed upon whose nerve he could place some reliance, my role was obvious. But apart from this I had uses. I was a whetstone for his mind. I stimulated him. He liked to think aloud in my presence. His remarks could hardly be said to be made to me – many of them would have been as appropriately addressed to his bedstead – but none the less, having formed the habit, it had become in some way helpful that I should register and interject. If I irritated him by a certain methodical slowness in my mentality, that irritation served only to make his own flamelike intuitions and impressions flash up more vividly and swiftly. Such was my humble role in our alliance.

This relationship was not, of course, confined to 'those latter days'. It just had not dawned on Watson until then.

The widespread popularity of Sherlock Holmes really dates from the series of short stories which Dr Arthur Conan Doyle began contributing to *The Strand Magazine* in 1891. The immediate success which these stories achieved gave Conan Doyle the great break he needed, and an insatiable demand of the public for more.

By the time twenty-four short stories had appeared, Conan Doyle had tired of Holmes and was anxious to get on with what he considered the more important work of his historical novels. So, in the story *The Final Problem*, he killed off his most famous figure in a death struggle with the arch-criminal Professor Moriarty at the Reichenbach Falls. Only then did Conan Doyle realise what a hold his character had on the public's imagination.

Like the monthly parts of Dickens's novels, each issue of *The Strand* had been eagerly awaited for the latest Sherlock Holmes adventure, with queues forming at bookstalls. When *The Final Problem* appeared, young City men went about with black crêpe on their hats and mourning bands on their arms. One woman, writing indignantly to Doyle, began her letter, 'You brute!' George Newnes, publisher of *The Strand*, described the demise of Sherlock Holmes to his shareholders as 'a dreadful event'.

What more favourable time could there have been to present a Sherlock Holmes play? The man who grasped the opportunity was

Charles Rogers, a minor dramatist of the period whose principal success up to that time had been a melodrama in the prevailing fashion of crime and detection entitled £1,000 Reward. In 1893 he wrote Sherlock Holmes, a lurid melodrama in the accepted style of the period. Rogers had crammed it full of exciting incidents, and had taken a number of liberties with his appropriated characters. Dr Watson is shown as having a wife, Amy, and a child, Lily. After Watson has mysteriously disappeared, we learn that Sherlock Holmes had once offered his love to Amy, who had refused him and accepted Watson. She reveals this when admonishing Holmes for his apparent slowness in tracing Watson, as she imagines that he wishes to take advantage of Watson's absence. Watson has been abducted by a maniac responsible for a series of diabolical murders on the lines of the Jack-the-Ripper killings. When Holmes finally locates Watson, he finds him deprived of memory as the result of a blow on the head. Rather than leave him to the mercy of the maniac, Wilton Hursher, Holmes plunges a hypodermic syringe into Watson and renders him to all intents and purposes lifeless. Holmes is promptly imprisoned for the murder of Watson, but escapes in time to prevent an autopsy on Watson, which, he discloses, would really kill him. He has only been rendered apparently dead for forty-eight hours by a rare Indian drug. The final scene shows Mrs Watson about to be killed by Hursher in full view of the audience, but he relents just in time and takes poison before he can be captured.

'Nervous people should not go to see Sherlock Holmes', wrote the Glasgow Evening Citizen, 'even though there are attempts at enlivenment in the course of the play.' Even now the play reads as very strong drama indeed.

The role of Hursher was a gift for the barn-storming actors of the time, for he dominated the action rather at the expense of the hero; an error of judgement that many important writers have made. But Charles Rogers was not a great playwright. He excelled in producing a number of dramas of popular appeal, and he must be admired for his astuteness in combining the already famous characters Sherlock Holmes and Dr Watson with an unsolved, real-life series of horrible crimes, still comparatively fresh in the minds of the public.

Under the copyright laws of the time Conan Doyle had virtually no protection against the use of his characters in stage plays. In fact,

Charles Rogers had secured for himself a playright (as it was then called) in his drama by a 'copyright performance' at Hanley in December 1893. This gave him the exclusive right to perform his play, just as Doyle's copyright gave him the exclusive right to have his stories printed. Rogers was safe so long as he did not use any passages or incidents from the stories, and he was obviously careful about that.

Even so, when a new Sherlock Holmes play was brought to England in 1901, there was a flurry of litigation as each party tried to prevent the other from competing. Charles Rogers was dead by then, but his successors sought to prevent another play being presented under the title *Sherlock Holmes*; they failed because there is no copyright in titles. Then the other side sought and obtained an injunction to stop the Charles Rogers play from being passed off as having anything to do with the Lyceum production. The injunction was not always observed.

But Charles Rogers's play had enjoyed a good life round the provinces, and was not in the same class as its competitor, which had been launched in equally favourable circumstances. The competitor was William Gillette's play *Sherlock Holmes*, first produced in England while the novel *The Hound of the Baskervilles* was appearing in serial form in *The Strand Magazine*. The young City men were rejoicing at the reappearance of their favourite, although their jubilation was tempered by the realisation that *The Hound* was described by the author as an adventure that had taken place before Sherlock Holmes's death.

CHAPTER 2

William Gillette

You make the poor hero of the anaemic printed page a very
limp object as compared with the glamour of your own
personality which you infuse into his stage presentment.

Conan Doyle to William Gillette

Conan Doyle eventually had to give in and revive Sherlock Holmes
(who apparently never really went over the falls but just pushed
Moriarty off). In the meantime, to stave off the demand for more
Holmes stories, Doyle wrote *The Hound of the Baskervilles*. It proved
to be one of the best-known and most popular of the stories.

But some years before, Conan Doyle had written a Sherlock Holmes
play which he had sent to Herbert Beerbohm Tree. It was typical of
Tree that he asked Doyle to rewrite the play to feature Beerbohm
Tree's idiosyncrasies rather than those of Sherlock Holmes, and Conan
Doyle was understandably reluctant to change his creation. He lost
interest in the idea, but his literary agent retrieved the play and sent it
to the American impresario Charles Frohman.

Frohman, then in his late thirties, was already one of the greatest
American theatrical managers, with a remarkable reputation for dis-
covering and developing theatrical talent. He helped to make stars of
such players as Ethel Barrymore, Billie Burke, Otis Skinner and
William Gillette, before he died in the Lusitania in 1915.

Among other plays, William Gillette had written and, under
Frohman's auspices, appeared in the hugely successful *Secret Service*,
one of the classic melodramas of the late nineteenth century. Charles
Frohman gave the Doyle play to Gillette who wrote to Conan Doyle
and obtained permission to rewrite it. Warming to the task of creating

a virtually new play, Gillette cabled to Doyle 'May I marry Holmes?' By this time Doyle had grown heartily sick of the whole business: 'You may marry or murder or do what you like with him,' was his laconic response.

Gillette was in California at the time, appearing in the farewell tour of *Secret Service*, and Frohman gave him leave of absence from the cast to complete the writing of his new play. A whiff of melodrama was detectable at the outset, for no sooner had Gillette completed the manuscript than it was lost in a San Francisco hotel fire. Undeterred, he wrote the whole play again, and then in May 1899 visited Conan Doyle in England to seek his approval. Doyle made no objections, and within a fortnight or so the play was given a copyright performance in London. Gillette returned to America to prepare for the production, little realising what he had embarked upon.

The story of the play mainly derives from two of Doyle's short stories, *A Scandal in Bohemia* and *The Final Problem*, both of which have since been used by other dramatists, for good and obvious reasons. From *A Scandal in Bohemia* comes the only slight trace of love interest ever evinced by Sherlock Holmes ('When he speaks of Irene Adler,' wrote Watson, 'it is always under the honourable title of *the* woman'), while from *The Final Problem* comes Professor Moriarty. Next to Sherlock Holmes and Dr Watson, Professor Moriarty is the best-known character in the whole Holmes saga, although he appears in only one story (and is referred to in two others). Stage and screen writers have seized on him enthusiastically for their adaptations, for Conan Doyle's notion of a master criminal – 'the Napoleon of crime' – as a worthy adversary for his master detective has never been surpassed.

Like a spider sitting at the centre of its web, Moriarty controls a vast underworld network of crime, and when Sherlock Holmes is finally hard on the Professor's heels there occurs a confrontation between the two master-minds that Conan Doyle depicts with admirable restraint: 'All that I have to say has already crossed your mind,' warns Moriarty. 'Then possibly my answer has crossed yours,' retorts Holmes. The encounter is lifted virtually straight from the story into the play, and in fact much of the play's dialogue can be found scattered among the stories. To the Holmesian the play is a bit like *Hamlet* – all quotations.

It is concerned with the recovery by Sherlock Holmes of a packet of letters, photographs and jewellery from Miss Alice Faulkner, who has fallen into the hands of Madge and James Larrabee, a scoundrelly couple bent on obtaining the package themselves. The Larrabees appeal for help to Professor Moriarty, who is only too eager to even up a few old scores. Moriarty visits Holmes at the Baker Street rooms, and the confrontation takes place.

When Moriarty's direct approach to Holmes fails, Holmes is lured to a Gas Chamber in Stepney, where he is to be disposed of. But Holmes not only outwits the gang sent to kill him, but also succeeds in trapping them in their own Gas Chamber.

The episode in the Gas Chamber is the least plausible part of the play. We are seriously expected to believe that four ruthless and determined men, three of them killers with instructions to kill, would stand and bandy words with a detective while he sits calmly smoking a cigar and writing a brief description of them for the benefit of the police. Perhaps they were taken aback by the ensuing dialogue:

> CRAIGIN You'd better look out Miss – he might get killed.
> ALICE Then you can kill me too.
> HOLMES I'm afraid you don't mean that, Miss Faulkner.
> ALICE Yes, I *do*.
> HOLMES No. You would not say it – at another time or place.
> ALICE I would say it anywhere – always.

This introduction of love interest, with its rather banal dialogue, tends to obscure an exciting piece of stage business that concludes the scene. Holmes smashes an oil lamp on the table and in the darkness the gang attempt to locate him by the glow of his cigar. When they restore the light they find he has fixed his cigar in the window frame and escaped through the door at the other side of the room, taking Alice with him.

In the final scene Moriarty is captured, and Holmes and Alice embrace in a pool of limelight as the curtain falls.

Sherlock Holmes opened in New York in November 1899, with William Gillette in the title role. It ran for 236 performances, after which Gillette toured the USA with the play until the summer of 1901. The company then sailed for England and, after a week's try-out at Liverpool, opened in London at the Lyceum Theatre on 9 September

1901. They brought with them an enormous load of electrical apparatus for creating the special lighting effects which excited as much comment as any other aspect of the production. After the first night in London *The Westminster Gazette* wrote: 'The darkness was quite the most brilliant novelty of the affair. Of course it is an old thing to have the stage darkened whilst the scenes are being changed; in the present instance, however, the stage management goes further. To begin an act the house was put into utter darkness and light gradually introduced, disclosing the scene; whilst to end each act darkness descended upon the stage gradually, and one or two pretty pictures came from this.'

Equally impressive, apparently, were the slick scene changes made during the brief spells of total darkness. The smooth efficiency of the whole presentation was a major factor in what was one of the great box-office hits of the early twentieth century. Yet the acting, and the play itself, came in for some very mixed receptions.

The critic of *The Westminster Gazette*, for example, continued his review with wry sarcasm: 'I should like to have spoken more enthusiastically concerning this authorised stage treatment of Dr. Conan Doyle's hero of many interesting and ingenious stories, but, unfortunately, the qualities that distinguish the book vanish – perhaps in the darkness preceding each act – the Sherlock Holmes of the stage is a mere burlesque of the Sherlock Holmes of the study.'

The drama critic of *The Daily Telegraph* (Malcolm Watson, who turns up again later) devoted two columns to a very thoughtful review, but could not avoid scoffing at the play and expressing disappointment at the performances: 'Sherlock Holmes is a serious artist – in grim, downright, deadly earnest every moment; and in the hands of Mr. William Gillette he loses nothing of his grimness. The performance of the American actor is, in many respects, interesting, though it is hardly great. In fact, there is a certain stiffness of monotony about it ... Mr. Gillette makes a sad, stern, almost smileless figure on the stage, and it is regretted that his suggestion of reserved force carried with it more than a suggestion of reserved voice.' (At the Lyceum first night Gillette was inaudible in some parts of the house, and after the final curtain members of the audience protested loudly. Gillette unwisely attempted a speech and rebuked the audience, which only added to the upset.)

The Times critic had his tongue firmly embedded in his cheek when he delivered his gently mocking appraisal: 'It would be a shame to tell the story, even if we completely understood it . . . the Napoleon of crime should have been above using a revolver casually left on the table by Sherlock Holmes. If he had ever seen a melodrama he would have known that the cartridges had been withdrawn.'

The Stage was much less amiable: 'Such measure of non-success as *Sherlock Holmes* was accorded [at the first night] was due, mainly, to Mr. Gillette's apparent failure to make his voice carry all over the house . . . and to the patent fact that *Sherlock Holmes* is, when reduced to essentials, nothing more than a crude and commonplace, though exciting, melodrama.'

Hardly the sort of reception to guarantee long runs, yet the successes of both Gillette and the play were even greater in England than in America. There were two clear indications of how celebrated Gillette became during this first run in London. Firstly, along with all the notabilities of the day, he was caricatured by Spy in *Vanity Fair*; secondly, there appeared a lively crop of parodies and music-hall sketches, mostly concerned with guying the Lyceum production. By far the most successful was the one written by Malcolm Watson (of the *Telegraph*) and Edward La Serre, called *Sheerluck Jones* or *Why D'Gillette Him Off?*

William Gillette's plays tended to be written for himself to star in, and none more so than *Sherlock Holmes*. Consequently, the title role is tailored to match the extremely cultured and dignified person that Gillette really was, and on the stage he was able to exercise a personal magnetism that made his audiences sublimely unconscious of the short-comings of the play.

Nearly a year before William Gillette's play reached England, there appeared at Clapham a melodrama entitled *The Bank of England*. It was written by Max Goldberg, a prolific writer of second-class melodramas that circulated among the many provincial theatres of that period.

The play was subtitled *An Adventure in the Life of Sherlock Holmes* and concerned the circulation of forged banknotes by two villainous directors of the Bank of England. A wealthy American lady receives a lot of the forgeries in her winnings at a race meeting and asks Sherlock Holmes to investigate. Fearing exposure, the two directors plan to abscond with bullion worth half a million pounds from the bank's vaults and in the course of their preparations they murder one of their accomplices – the forger. Sherlock Holmes utilises several disguises during the play; apart from that of an old gentleman from India, he turns up as the captain of the bank guard and, at the climax of the melodrama, he appears as the ghost of the murdered forger and extracts a full confession of all the crimes. Goldberg himself played Sherlock Holmes, under his stage name of John F. Preston. The play was certainly well received by the public, for it toured steadily for seven years or more.

William Gillette's play *Sherlock Holmes* remained at the Lyceum until April 1902, by which time there were four touring companies taking the play round the country, and when the Lyceum run closed, Gillette and his company toured Britain before returning to America. This period in 1902 was the most triumphant spell of Sherlock Holmes on the stage in Britain. Apart from the Lyceum company on the road, there were Charles Frohman's North and South principal touring companies, as well as two of Ben Greet's touring companies, all giving the William Gillette play, together with a company performing Charles Rogers's play and a company performing *The Bank of England* – in all, seven companies touring simultaneously in Sherlock Holmes plays!

Meanwhile, overseas productions were mounted, complete with all the special effects of course, in Holland, Russia, Denmark and Sweden. Prior to the authorised production in Denmark, the Danish author Walter Christmas had seen the play in New York. As Frohman's price for the rights was considered too high, Christmas made notes on his cuffs during several performances and wrote a play in Danish based on what he had seen and remembered. It ran in Copenhagen for five months and remained in the theatre's repertoire for three years. Similarly in Sweden, it was a translation of Walter Christmas's play that stole the thunder from the authorised translation; on one evening in 1902 it was performed at three different Stockholm theatres simultaneously.

In England, Charles Frohman's North Company had H. A. Saintsbury as Sherlock Holmes, while the South Company had Julian Royce. Their places were subsequently filled over the years by a succession of other leading players. Of all the English actors who portrayed Sherlock

Holmes on the stage, H. A. Saintsbury was by far the most successful, appearing in the role hundreds of times in plays as well as in a film.

Julian Royce, while not so successful as Saintsbury, was nevertheless a very impressive Holmes and he too toured in the Gillette play for a number of years, and also resumed the role when *The Speckled Band* touring companies started in 1910.

When the North Company started on their second tour of *Sherlock Holmes* in July 1903, H. A. Saintsbury took with him in the cast the most celebrated person ever to play Billy the page-boy – twelve year old Master Charles Chaplin. In the very moving section of his autobiography dealing with his childhood and early life in London, Mr Chaplin sets his casting in the role of Billy against the poignant background of his family's crushing poverty and ill-fortune, and describes the overwhelming effect of receiving this, his first stage engagement, for the salary of £2 10s per week. A perceptive reviewer of his first week's performance wrote: 'A faithful portrait of Billy is given by Master Charles Chaplin, who shows considerable ability, and bids fair to develop into a capable and clever actor.'

Following this promising start, the favourable comments on the portrayal of Billy were numerous. Scarcely a week passed without a mention: 'Master Charles Chaplin makes a smart little Billy', 'Billy is well played by Master Charles Chaplin', 'Master Charles Chaplin (a capital Billy)', and so on. Chaplin's brother Sydney joined the company in a small role and the two of them continued to tour in the play, with minor breaks, until March 1906.

A decade later, in an interview given in California, Charlie Chaplin, then the highest-paid movie star in the world, recalled his stage début with some affection:

> People always connect me and my work with my training under Fred Karno the vaudeville manager on the other side; but as a matter of fact, I owe more to the tutelage of a Mr. Saintsbury, who gave me my first legitimate engagement as Billy, the boy in *Sherlock Holmes*, than to anybody in the world.

In September 1905, William Gillette came to London with the beautiful Marie Doro to present his play *Clarice*. He decided to put on with it, as a curtain-raiser, a one-act play that he had performed at a benefit in New York earlier that year – *The Painful Predicament of Sherlock Holmes.*

Gillette's stage manager wired to the provinces for Charles Chaplin to play Billy at the Duke of York's Theatre – the West End at last! ('I trembled with anxiety,' wrote Chaplin, 'for it was doubtful if our company could replace Billy in the provinces on such short notice.') But they did.

Apart from Chaplin as Billy and Gillette as Holmes, the only other member of the cast was Irene Vanbrugh, who played Miss Gwendolyn Cobb, the lady who calls on Holmes and talks so much that he is unable to utter a word. She drops his tobacco jar, treads on his violin, sits on the bow, smashes a chemistry retort and knocks over a lamp, all without a break in the ceaseless flow of chatter. Holmes is finally saved when two warders arrive to take the lady back to the asylum.

But Chaplin's triumph seemed short-lived, for after thirteen performances the theatre closed; *Clarice* was a flop. To salvage the season, William Gillette decided to reopen the very next week with a revival of *Sherlock Holmes*, which he had revived earlier in the year in New York.

'*Sherlock Holmes* was received with rapture,' reported *The Stage*, 'Mr. Gillette had to take many calls after act three and at the end of the performance.' It was a very successful revival, with a number of royal visitors during the seven-week run and, of course, 'Master Charles Chaplin is capital as the faithful page, Billy.'

An Adventure in the Life of Sherlock Holmes was originally presented as a 'sketch in two episodes' by John Lawson, who played Sherlock Holmes in it round the London music halls early in 1902. But in spite of a note on his playbill stating 'This is NOT from the Lyceum Theatre', Lawson fell foul of Charles Frohman's solicitors, who were vigorously hunting down every little music-hall sketch and playlet that was using the name Sherlock Holmes in the title or publicity.

However, some arrangement must have been made, for in May 1902 John Lawson's piece reappeared, considerably enlarged, as 'an episode in three scenes'. Amazingly, the plot seems to have been far more of a crib from Gillette's play than the original sketch, right up to the equivalent of the Gas Chamber scene, only this time it is the laboratory of the villain, Baron de Denmar. The baron sets going the machine which was the sensation of the music-hall sketch – a gramophone that plays sweet music and emits poisonous gas from the horn at the same time. The report in *The Stage* tells the rest in an incomparable manner:

> Sylvester (the heroine) now faints, and de Denmar is just escaping with the documents when Sherlock Holmes makes his appearance and bars the way. Sylvester recovers and Holmes demands the letters. The answer from de Denmar is four shots from his revolver at Holmes, but owing to a mailed shirt which he always wears, he is unhurt. They are all more or less getting suffocated, and de Denmar is compelled to turn the machine off. A struggle ensues between de Denmar and Holmes, in which Holmes secures the papers. De Denmar in his rage says: 'You shall not escape me, even if I have to perish.' He then hurls a chair at a lighted lamp, and the globe being smashed a terrific explosion occurs, and de Denmar perishes in the ruins, Holmes and Sylvester just making their escape in the nick of time.

Charles Frohman's lawyers were in action again in New York in 1903, when a four-act version of *The Sign of the Four* was staged. This time not even Conan Doyle's original story was copyright in the USA, and after several hearings the injunction was denied on those grounds. The play, written by Charles P. Rice, was well-received without being a big success, and like a number of Sherlock Holmes plays it kept on touring for years. As late as 1912 it was given by a stock company at the Grand Theatre, San Diego, California, with a young Harold Lloyd in the part of Tonga, the little East Indian whose activities with a blowpipe and poisoned darts put Sherlock Holmes on to the trail of the Agra treasure. An earlier American play based on *The Sign of Four* had been successfully stopped by a Chicago court in 1901, but then the Frohman team apparently had a stronger case. The play was entitled *Sherlock Holmes, Detective: or The Sigh of the Four*, and could have been mistaken for Gillette's play.

In 1907 there appeared the most unusual variant of the Gillette play, written by Pierre Decourcelle, who transformed it into a French play. The production became the talk of Paris, and enjoyed an enormous success. Decourcelle renamed about half the characters, including Sid Prince, the safe-cracker employed by the Larrabees, whom he called John Alfred Napoleon Bribb, and, at the point at which Gillette's play ends, it is Bribb who has the darbies snapped onto his wrists by Holmes.

So Moriarty is left free for a dénouement of great imagination. The curtain rises on a stage divided into three, with Dr Watson's house on the left, a street in the middle, and the Empty House on the right, and thus Decourcelle wrings the additional drama from yet another Doyle story, with the attempted shooting of Sherlock Holmes from across the street by Moriarty, who is apprehended after shooting the dummy Holmes has placed in the window. (In the story *The Empty House* Moriarty has already perished, so it is Colonel Moran who is caught in this situation.)

But as well as extra scenes, Decourcelle had rewritten the play in a French style with many slight changes and subtle Gallicisms that give it a distinctive Parisian flavour. In the Gillette original, for example, Larrabee returns home and warns his wife: 'They've put Holmes on the case.' 'Sherlock Holmes?' she asks. 'Yes,' replies Larrabee. In the Decourcelle version she responds at greater length: 'Sherlock Holmes? Le détective amateur dont tout l'Europe célèbre la perspicacité? Celui qui a découvert les voleurs du wagon-poste Calais-Brindisi et divine que le véritable coupable dans l'affaire des diamants de Lady Melrose, c'était elle-même pour payer les dettes de jeu de son ami.' To which her husband exclaims, 'Parbleu! Comme s'il y en avait un autre.'

Decourcelle delighted in sprinkling English names all over the play for 'authenticity'. When Professor Moriarty is planning to visit Sherlock Holmes, he enquires: 'C'est, je crois, dans Baker Street qu'il demeure?', and is told 'Oui, Monsieur, 123 Baker Street . . . au coin de la petite ruelle de Throgmorton.'

Decourcelle may well have purloined the idea of the Empty House episode from a German play of a year earlier, written and performed by Ferdinand Bonn, proprietor of the Berliner Theater in Berlin. Bonn's play, *Sherlock Holmes*, was largely an unauthorised copy of Gillette's play, with liberal doses of heavy German humour provided by two absurd police inspectors. This Laurel-and-Hardy pair, named Knox and Smallweed, turned up again the following year in Ferdinand Bonn's *Der Hund von Baskerville*, which was stated to be 'aus Poes und Doyles Novellen'. The setting was changed from Dartmoor to the Scottish Highlands so that the buried treasure of Bonnie Prince Charlie could be added to a story that was generally on the lines of Conan Doyle's novel, *The Hound of the Baskervilles*. The connection with

Edgar Allan Poe was presumably the locating of the buried treasure by measurements from a tree, taken from Poe's *The Gold Bug*. *Der Hund von Baskerville* was a considerable improvement on Bonn's first Sherlock Holmes play; the tiresome comic interludes were much shorter and less frequent, although the dialogue had some long-winded philosophical arguments which ruined the dramatic tension inherent in the original story.

MASTER CHARLES CHAPLIN,
Sherlock Holmes Co.
Disengaged March 5th.
Coms., 9, Tavistock Place. Tele., 2,187 Hop.

The Stage (1 March 1906)

All the while, in the English provinces, the tours of the William Gillette play went on and on, visiting towns as many as four and five times, and there were very few breaks until the mid-1920s. Back in America, Gillette himself appeared in further revivals in 1906, 1910 and 1915. Then in March 1916, the Essanay Film Company, employers of that same Charles Chaplin, announced to the Press that they had signed William Gillette to appear in film versions of his well-known plays *Sherlock Holmes* and *Secret Service*. Production began immediately and *Sherlock Holmes* was released in the USA, to the accompaniment of ecstatic reviews, in May 1916. As things turned out, the film of *Secret Service* was never made and *Sherlock Holmes* was Gillette's only film. He was then sixty-three years old, and the American magazine *Moving Picture World* was alert to the historical worth of the film:

A few more years and it would have become impossible for Mr. Gillette to take his part with the physical vigour that would recall his best efforts of the old days to his international-wide admirers, and at the same time leave in comparatively permanent form his Sherlock Holmes for the delight of future generations.

Unfortunately, nobody else was alert to the value of that film, and no copy has survived. It would have provided a remarkable visual record of the great actor's most famous role.

All this time Conan Doyle, considerably better off thanks to the persistent popularity of Sherlock Holmes, had achieved a large output of stories, books and plays, not all of them successful.

At the end of 1909, Doyle staged an elaborately dramatised version of his boxing novel *Rodney Stone*, retitled *The House of Temperley*, at the Adelphi Theatre, London. Because no management would risk such an ambitious production, Doyle had backed it out of his own pocket, leasing the Adelphi for six months, but after a promising start the play went badly and closed.

> When I saw the course that things were taking I shut myself up and devoted my whole mind to making a sensational Sherlock Holmes drama. I wrote it in a week and called it 'The Speckled Band' after the short story of that name . . . Before the end of the run I had cleared off all that I had lost upon the other play, and I had created a permanent property of some value.

Less than a month after *The House of Temperley* came off, *The Speckled Band* opened, and was warmly received.

The original short story *The Speckled Band* related how Helen Stoner consults Sherlock Holmes at Baker Street about the mysterious death of her sister two years previously. She now fears for her own life. Holmes undertakes to investigate and arranges to visit the family home at Stoke Moran. Hardly has Miss Stoner left when her angry stepfather bursts into Holmes's room and warns him not to meddle. Unknown to the stepfather, Dr Grimesby Roylott, Holmes and Watson travel to Stoke Moran, examine the house and hide themselves in Miss Stoner's room. When they hear the strange sounds of which she was frightened, Holmes strikes at a snake coming down the bell-rope and drives it back through the ventilator, where it turns on its master, Roylott, and kills him. Holmes had already deduced that Roylott had killed Julia Stoner, the sister, with the snake and that he planned to kill Helen in the same way.

The stage play follows the general line of this short story, but the treatment of characters and incidents differs considerably and there are also some changes of the principal names.

Within four months of the opening night, two touring companies were sent out while the London production continued. Next to William Gillette's play, Conan Doyle's *The Speckled Band* is the best-known

Sherlock Holmes stage play. Yet its success was almost as much due to the villain of the piece as to the famous detective, for not only had Doyle depicted Dr Grimesby Roylott as an overpowering character but also Lyn Harding, who created and played the role over many years, dominated the play with his impressive stature and his vigorous barn-storming acting. Doyle acknowledged his own responsibility for the results: 'The real fault of this play was that in trying to give Holmes a worthy antagonist I overdid it and produced a more interesting personality in the villain. The terrible ending was also against it.'

In reworking his short story into a drama, Conan Doyle had made some drastic alterations. The most serious was the exaggeration of Dr Roylott. Even in the short story Roylott was a larger-than-life villain, but at least Sherlock Holmes was shown to be his equal. In the play Roylott looms large while Holmes is diminished to little more than an ordinary character, and the balance in the story is missing on the stage. The play is subtitled *An Adventure of Sherlock Holmes* (clearly an asset when it came to publicity), but Holmes does not make an appearance until the second scene of Act II, when the play is half over. Moreover, the majority of observations and deductions which put Sherlock Holmes on the track of the criminal (and which he makes for himself in the short story) are made in the play by two other characters. To add to the humiliation, one of these is Dr Watson!

The obvious choice for the role of Holmes was H. A. Saintsbury. After years as a touring actor he had finally 'arrived' in the London theatre world; another example of how portraying Sherlock Holmes has affected an actor's career.

Saintsbury was a very gentlemanly dignified Holmes, modelled on William Gillette's performances, and he made it his most celebrated role. 'Mr. H. A. Saintsbury,' wrote *The Times*, 'seems to have been born to play Sherlock Holmes – always imperturbable, glib and, as the French say, "somebody".'

As well as playing the villain, Dr Roylott, Lyn Harding was also engaged to produce the play. According to Hesketh Pearson, there was a disagreement at rehearsals between Harding and Conan Doyle as to how Dr Roylott should be played. Harding wanted to emphasise the neurotic side of the character, and, upon the advice of James Barrie, Doyle finally gave way. It is difficult to judge who was right. Certainly

Harding achieved a great success with his characterisation, although even as it is written the part of Dr Roylott seems heavy enough, without any exaggeration in the playing. He continued to play the role in tours following the original production, and again in 1921 when the play was revived.

In spite of the growing competition from the cinema, and the counter-attraction of *The Speckled Band*, William Gillette's *Sherlock Holmes* still had some distance to go. There were revivals in America in 1923 and 1928, and finally, in 1929, Gillette emerged from retirement at the age of seventy-six and began a farewell tour of the USA in the play. It was not so much a tour as a royal progress, and was given a great send-off at the first night in New York by the leaders of American society, academicians and notabilities from many fields; on stage after the final curtain, Professor Lyon Phelps of Yale University conferred on Gillette an MA degree, and read congratulatory letters from former President Calvin Coolidge and other eminent Americans.

Gillette's reception was so overwhelming that it was three seasons later, in March 1932, before he eventually completed the tour. During this period he also became the first-ever radio Sherlock Holmes when he launched a series of half-hour programmes in 1930.

Even after his astonishing farewell tour he had not quite finished; in 1935 he and many of the members of the tour company performed a broadcast of his play for CBS on the Lux Radio Theatre, just two years before he died.

CHAPTER 3

The Earliest Films

> The glamour in which our imaginations have enshrouded
> Sherlock Holmes cannot be captivated and presented in a film
> – or for that matter in a stage play.
>
> *Kinematograph Weekly* (1913)

When the first moviegoers had tired of actuality films of trains
entering and leaving stations, comic films of watering the gardener,
and the trick films of Melies and his contemporaries, they began to
expect a little more for their money. Film makers began to construct
small story films, of which *The Great Train Robbery* is perhaps the
most famous example.

Just as with television today, the early cinema consumed material
at an alarming rate and it was not long before stories by well-known
authors were being plundered for ideas and plots, both before and
after copyright protection came into being. Stories and characters
which have already acquired a reputation are naturally better box-office
attractions.

It was as early as 1900 that Sherlock Holmes made his screen début
and it was such a fleeting appearance as to be almost unnoticeable. The
film was *Sherlock Holmes Baffled*, made for viewing on a peep-show
machine. It runs for some forty-nine seconds and shows a dressing-
gowned figure entering a room to find a burglar busily filling his sack.
By means of trick photography the burglar disappears and reappears
several times, finally departing through the window with his swag, to
leave, in the words of the title, Sherlock Holmes baffled.

One might well wonder what this tiny film incident has to do with
Sherlock Holmes. The appearance of the dressing-gowned character

was clearly modelled on Gillette's celebrated portrayal of Holmes, and the film was a mildly amusing little piece, easily understood by the general public of the day. It is important only in that it marks the first use on film of the name and the character Sherlock Holmes.

The next recorded screen appearance was *The Adventures of Sherlock Holmes* or *Held for a Ransom*, made in the USA by Vitagraph in 1905. It was the first Sherlock Holmes film to be shown in England, when it formed part of the programme given at the Alhambra Theatre, London, in 1906. This film made some attempt to depict Sherlock Holmes in action as a detective, in a story claimed to be based on *The Sign of Four*.

After this, scarcely a year passed without Sherlock Holmes appearing on the screen somewhere in the world, even if only in the title. For instance, *A Case for Sherlock Holmes* (Cricks & Martin, 1911) had nothing whatsoever to do with Holmes, but the title was a box-office draw. When Sherlock Holmes actually appeared in a movie, he was very little different from any other screen sleuths of the time. Detective roles demanded an ability to solve crimes by a combination of intuition and luck, plus a fantastic acrobatic prowess for all the numerous fights, and inexhaustible stamina for chase after chase.

The first big landmark among silent Sherlock Holmes films was the series made by the Nordisk company in Denmark. This was at the time of an extraordinary eruption of talent in the Danish film industry that overflowed into pre-Great War Germany and drifted on into post-Great War Hollywood.

Between 1908 and 1911, Nordisk made eleven identifiable Sherlock Holmes films, with such titles as *Sherlock Holmes in the Gas Cellar*, *The Black Hand* and *Sherlock Holmes in the Claws of the Confidence Men*. Some of the adventures were as lurid as these titles suggest, but in general the films were well made for their time and some of them even contained recognisable incidents and characters from the Conan Doyle stories. Indeed, one of them, *The Grey Lady* (1909), followed quite closely the story line of Doyle's novel *The Hound of the Baskervilles*, except that instead of a ghostly hound, it was a ghostly lady that the villain was using to frighten the life out of the relatives who stood between him and the family inheritance.

The Nordisk series began with Sherlock Holmes pitted against two

Page 33 (left) William Gillette in the first New York production of his play *Sherlock Holmes* —scene in the Gas Chamber; (below) Viggo Larsen as Holmes, supported by dubious policemen, in one of the first Nordisk Sherlock Holmes films (1908–9)

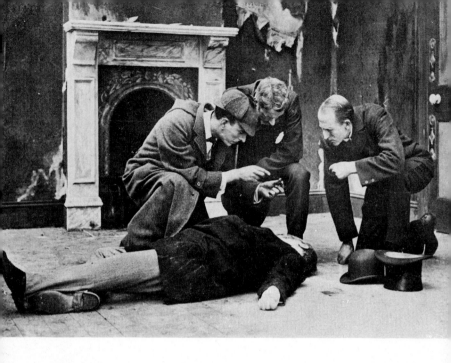

Page 34 (above) Holmes, Watson and Lestrade in a scene from *A Study in Scarlet* (Samuelson, 1914) that appears utterly faithful to the original story; (below) Sherlock Holmes (Alwin Neuss) treads warily in *Ein Schrei in der Nacht* (Decla, 1915)

master criminals – Moriarty and Raffles! In a story loosely based on part of William Gillette's play, Raffles is hard-pressed by Holmes and seeks the aid of Moriarty, who attempts to do away with Holmes, and ends up in prison for his pains. When the film, named *Sherlock Holmes*, reached America, the *New York Dramatic Mirror* gave it a lengthy and appreciative review.

> This picture had its first American presentation at the Fourteenth Street Theatre last week, and offered an excellent opportunity to compare the work of the Danish film pantomimists with that of moving picture actors of other countries. The comparison is not, by any means, to the disadvantage of the Danes. The photography of the film is of a superior quality, and the scenic effects quite ingenious and novel. The plot is also interesting and is developed with considerable skill and with reasonable lucidity, although it might have been made a little more clear in the early scenes. Too much, perhaps, is left to the spectator's knowledge regarding the personalities of Sherlock Holmes, Raffles and Moriarty. Nevertheless the story holds the attention strongly. The acting appears oddly stiff compared to that of French and American players, but it is most pleasantly devoid of the ridiculous overacting and contortions resorted to by so many pantomimists. When Raffles is arrested, he does not throw a succession of acrobatic fits and when Moriarty is taken, he is only reasonably violent in the hands of the officer. In short, if we may judge all Copenhagen pictures by this one, the issues of the Great Northern Company should prove welcome variations to any picture programme.

The sequel which promptly followed was (perhaps inevitably) entitled *Raffles Escapes from Prison*. There is a remarkably close similarity between this pair of Nordisk films and a pair of Spanish stage plays performed in Madrid. Both the films and the plays featured Holmes and Raffles in similar adventures, and both pairs appeared in 1908. The resemblance is too strong to be mere coincidence, and on the slender evidence available, plus the fact that the earliest film makers were shameless filchers of other people's material, it seems that the plays were first.

In another Nordisk film, *The Theft of the Diamonds* (1910), Sherlock Holmes was obliged to surmount some extraordinary difficulties, according to part of the synopsis:

> Sherlock Holmes, after hearing the name and scream through the telephone, remembers at once the address of the well-known singer, and drives to the

house as quickly as possible. He sees at once what has been done, and without hesitating he climbs up the rope to follow the thief. The latter cuts the rope, but Sherlock Holmes arrests him after a hot pursuit over several roofs of houses, etc.

Although none of the Nordisk films has survived, the stills, synopses and reviews that still exist indicate that the reputation of this set of films was probably well deserved. They were shown in Germany, England and the USA with great success, for silent films were a truly international commodity that only needed the subtitles changing to be enjoyed anywhere. Viggo Larsen, one of Nordisk's leading actors, wrote, directed and played Holmes in the first six Nordisk films, in 1908 and 1909, after which he went to Germany and joined the Vitascope company in Berlin.

When romantic villains or crook-heroes like Raffles or Arsène Lupin are about, the forces of law and order tend to get booed and hissed at as tyrants, and Maurice Leblanc, who created Arsène Lupin, discovered that this happens particularly when the master criminal is battling with a master detective. Leblanc's idea of matching Arsène Lupin against Sherlock Holmes was used by Vitascope in a series of five films called *Arsène Lupin versus Sherlock Holmes*, directed by Viggo Larsen and issued in 1910 and 1911. Larsen again played Holmes and the series was a great success. It was not until the last film, of course, that right finally triumphed over wrong and Lupin perished.

The second film of the series, *The Blue Diamond*, provides another illuminating synopsis. A girl accomplice of Lupin has stolen a valuable diamond ring and has planted a copy on Baron B. in an attempt to frame him.

He calls up his friend Sherlock Holmes, the great detective. The latter hands the ring back saying it is an imitation, and his friend the Baron innocent. The detective now searches the Baron's room and finds a door leading out into the garden. As he steps out a girl passes, and quickly the detective follows her. She hails a taxi and drives off, while Holmes clings on behind. Arriving at the house, she dismisses the man and enters. Then Holmes, disguising himself, apparently falls in a faint by the gate, where he is found by two men, who help him into the house. They inform the girl, who recognizing Holmes, telephones to her sweetheart that Holmes has arrived. Meantime the girl returns, he takes off his disguise and forces her to accompany him. Hailing a passing taxi, he and his fair companion enter, but here Arsène Lupin's skill in disguise is evident. The driver of the taxi is none other than the great criminal, and Holmes is driven to the quay, where he is confided to the care of the captain of a steam yacht, with instructions to take Holmes to England, and there set him free at a certain time. Holmes has been bound but turns the hands of the clock by his feet. Then he secures the captain's watch and puts the hands on. Apparently at the stated time Holmes is put ashore, but the little trick helps him, for he just catches a return boat. Arsène Lupin has made preparations to leave his house, when Sherlock Holmes appears. Lupin thrusts the girl behind a secret panel, and is marched off. But he regains his freedom by strategy, and with the help of friends leaves the prison. Sherlock Holmes prepares for his home journey. At the station an old grizzled porter takes his luggage. Then as the train slowly steams out, the porter, whipping off false hair and beard, discloses the well-known features of Arsène Lupin, and mockingly cries 'Bon voyage' after the baffled detective.

By the time the makers reached the end of this thrilling film they seemed to have forgotten how they started. Of course, the movie audiences of 1910 would be in a dither of excitement about it all, but we blasé people of today are more familiar with movie dramas and can't help wondering what became of the diamond and that girl thrust behind the secret panel.

At the same time as the Vitascope films began appearing, Nordisk resumed their Sherlock Holmes series, either by coincidence or by way of retaliation, with various actors as Holmes, including Alwin Neuss. Like Larsen, Neuss also went to Germany, where he too played Holmes again in later films.

A series of films featuring the same characters was a favourite device amongst film makers for several very good reasons. The basic unit of the cinema in the early days was the 1,000ft reel of film, which ran for approximately ten minutes, and programmes were made up of half-, one- or two-reel subjects.

The distributors and exhibitors firmly believed that a two-reel film was the absolute maximum length that patrons would tolerate, and until about 1914 they resisted most attempts to expose audiences to the rigours of the multi-reel films that certain eccentrics, particularly Europeans, seemed determined to produce.

Having to work within this arbitrary limitation of time caused the

Only One Producer in the World
Could Obtain It.

Only One Producer in the World
Could Perfect It.

Eclair Obtained and Perfected

"SHERLOCK HOLMES"

By Sir Arthur Conan Doyle

The Greatest Detective Tale in the World

The Most Thrilling Character in Literature.

Magnificently Produced in Five Features

TWO REELS

Remember the Success of "Zigomar"! "Sherlock Holmes" is the Sensational Triumph of Eclair's Classic Productions.

Wire and Write at Once for Exclusive State Rights

Universal Features
7 East 14th Street, New York City

Universal Features, a subsidiary of Eclair, placed this advertisement in the American *Moving Picture World* before the shooting of the series had even begun

film industry to think of other means of maintaining the cinemagoers' interest and of keeping down production costs. A serial or a series of films with a comparatively regular cast and production team was an ideal way of attaining both these ends, and consequently serials and series experienced a golden age between 1910 and 1930. Many companies produced series featuring their pet detective characters, many of whom were in competition with, or obvious imitations of, Sherlock Holmes. The French company, Eclipse, who produced a Nat Pinkerton series, acknowledged in an advertisement that 'the Nat Pinkerton series bids fair to set a standard in filmed detective stories similar to that which Sir Conan Doyle has achieved in regard to written ones'. After this disarming gesture they released an impudent film in which Nat Pinkerton is shown triumphing over his rivals Sherlock Holmes, Nick Carter and Nick Winter, who are all subjected to the ignominy of having to acknowledge Nat Pinkerton as their master.

By 1911 copyright legislation in several countries had begun to include motion pictures and consequently film makers were not able to make so free with authors' characters and stories, not without due acknowledgement and payment, that is. Conan Doyle made a deal with the French film company Eclair for the film rights of some of the short stories for a sum which he regarded as treasure trove, although later he had to pay ten times the amount to get the rights back.

Using the Kursaal at Bexhill-on-Sea for their studio interiors, Eclair made eight two-reel films with a cast that was all British save for the remarkable exception of Sherlock Holmes himself, who was played by a French actor, Georges Treville.

These eight films were released in the USA in 1912 and were not shown in England until 1913, by which time a ninth had been added to the series, *Sherlock Holmes Solves the Sign of the Four*, made in the USA by the Thanhouser Company.

These were the first Sherlock Holmes films authorised by Conan Doyle and the widespread publicity they were given placed great emphasis on the claim that they were made under the personal supervision of the author. There is no direct evidence of any actual involvement by Doyle; not even any chatty interviews with the Famous Author visiting Bexhill to witness the filming of his Celebrated Sleuth. But it is clear from the synopses that Eclair were required to keep fairly closely to the plots of the original stories. Even so, it comes as something of a shock to learn that in the first film of the series, *The Speckled Band*, Sherlock Holmes poses as Juanes Rilto, 'a foreigner of good position', and presents himself at the villain's country house, to ask for the hand of his stepdaughter. It is even more of a shock to learn that Dr Watson was omitted from the film altogether!

It is strange that in his memoirs Conan Doyle referred only to the French company's films and made no mention of a major film event that took place in 1914, only six months after the last of the Eclair series had appeared in England. The event was the first Sherlock Holmes film made by a British company and the first film version of *A Study in Scarlet*. By this time feature films had increased in length so that it was more convenient to make reasonable screen versions of celebrated works of literature and fiction.

In the spring of 1914 a young Birmingham film renter, fired with the success of a film he had sponsored, decided to form his own film company. His name was G. B. Samuelson, his age twenty-six. He acquired Worton Hall, Isleworth, with nine acres of ground, and engaged George Pearson as his film director. Pearson, aged thirty-nine, had given up a promising career in education two years earlier to enter the film industry, and eventually achieved a considerable reputation in British pictures between the wars. His work showed a sense of craftsmanship and depth of thought that was lacking in many of his contemporaries. The company's first film was to be *A Study in Scarlet*, the first of the Sherlock Holmes stories.

Within a month of acquisition, a glass studio had been built in the grounds of Worton Hall, and filming began in this studio in July. Filming of exteriors and locations had already been going on for a month at the Cheddar Gorge and Southport Sands. The former served as the Rockies while the latter represented the Salt Lake plains, and an exceedingly skilful depiction of the great Mormon trek was achieved.

Before the studio work had been fully completed the energetic Samuelson had already started his team on another project, and, in the midst of the frantic whirl of events that comprised early film making, there came the sudden shock of the outbreak of war.

Everything else was forgotten in the wave of jingoism that followed, and Samuelson and his company plunged straight into making *The*

Great European War, before the war was barely two months old! After another month or two things settled down to something nearer normal – whatever that meant in the film world – and in October 1914 *A Study in Scarlet* finally had its trade showing in London.

The cinema press were extremely generous with their praise, devoting whole-page reviews to the film: 'Every advantage has been taken by the producer of the melodramatic episodes of *A Study in Scarlet,* with the result that the film, without slavishly following the book, nevertheless gains very considerably from the skilful manner in which the story has been handled.' Particular praise was given to the realism of George Pearson's production: 'the atmosphere – of crime, Scotland Yard, suburban life and sleuth hounds – is subtly reproduced and proves how admirably the producers have caught the spirit of their theme'.

In his autobiography, *Flashback,* George Pearson gives a fascinating insight into the casting of the great detective:

> Sherlock Holmes was a problem: much depended upon his physical appearance, build, height, and mannerisms had to be correct. By a remarkable stroke of fortune Samuelson had an employee in his Birmingham office who absolutely fitted these requirements, and as in those days of silent technique, a tactful producer could control every action of an inexperienced actor, I decided to risk his engagement as the shrewd detective. With his long and lean figure, his deer-stalker hat, cape-coat and curved pipe, he looked the part, and played the part excellently.

The man was Samuelson's accountant. His name was James Bragington and he never appeared in any other film.

Samuelson achieved another Holmesian 'first' in 1916 – the first film version of *The Valley of Fear* – and this time he shrewdly engaged as Sherlock Holmes an actor who had already played the role on the stage more than one thousand times – H. A. Saintsbury. Even without the obvious attraction of Saintsbury as Holmes, the film would have been successful, for it was another extremely well-made visual drama of murder and implacable revenge that followed the same pattern as *A Study in Scarlet.*

It was Saintsbury's only venture into film acting, and his comments made at the time indicated that he was not very comfortable in the medium:

In acting on the stage, one has carefully prepared the part. For the film, the acting has to be spontaneous. Acting for the film is the art of panto-mime, and every actor ought to be able to express without words exactly what he feels; but it is very difficult to do it on the spur of the moment, and I have never felt so selfconscious in my life as at my screen debut. I felt I could have acted the part much better if I had had half-an-hour to think about it.

Studying the scenario does not help much, because for screen production everything depends on the producer. There may be ten minutes of rehearsal, and before you know where you are, you are taken. The character of Sher-lock Holmes, with his 'inscrutable' face and passive attitude, was specially difficult to adapt to the film; I had to do just the things I had left out on the stage.

At exactly the same time, in Hollywood, a certain Charlie Chaplin, with nearly fifty films behind him, was acknowledging his indebted-ness to Saintsbury, to whom he could have given all the guidance needed with the problems of screen acting.

Both Samuelson productions were exceptional films in a period when the British film industry was badly hit by the effects of the Great War. Only the most outstanding films stood any chance of competing with the enormous output of the American studios.

It was no coincidence that in 1914 another *A Study in Scarlet* was released in the USA, for advance news of Samuelson's project had reached Los Angeles long before his film was ready. Certainly by 1914 standards Samuelson's film was a long time in the making, and in fact the two-reel version made by the Gold Seal Company was released in America the day after Samuelson's film was released in England. The scenario was by Grace Cunard and the film, directed by Francis Ford, was one of the large number of detective, secret service and adventure two-reelers that were being made by Francis Ford and Grace Cunard at that time. They frequently played the leading roles as well, and on this occasion Francis Ford (elder brother of the director, John Ford) duly appeared as Sherlock Holmes. Judging from the only available photograph it was very much an early Hollywood notion of Holmes, in an American-style cloth cap and garish check dressing-gown, worn together!

One of the most surprising demonstrations of the widespread fame of Sherlock Holmes was made in Germany during the Great War, at a time when one would expect anything English to have been very much out of favour.

Siegfried Kracauer, in an absorbing history of German films entitled *From Caligari to Hitler*, makes some interesting comments on the status of the detective film in Germany.

> The first German master detective to be serialized was Ernst Reicher as eagle-eyed Stuart Webbs, who, with the peaked cap and the inevitable shag pipe, had all the trade marks of Sherlock Holmes. Since he enjoyed an immense popularity, he was soon followed by competitors vainly trying to outdo him. They called themselves 'Joe Deebs' or 'Harry Higgs', were on excellent terms with Scotland Yard, and lived up to their English names by looking exactly like tailor-made gentlemen.
>
> It is noteworthy that, while the French and Americans succeeded in creating a national counterpart of Conan Doyle's archetype, the Germans always conceived of the great detective as an English character. This may be explained by the dependence of the classic detective upon liberal democracy. He, the single-handed sleuth who makes reason destroy the spider webs of irrational powers and decency triumph over dark instincts, is the predestined hero of a civilised world which believes in the blessings of enlightenment and individual freedom. It is not accidental that the sovereign detective is disappearing today in films and novels alike, giving way to the tough 'private investigator': the potentialities of liberalism seem, temporarily, exhausted. Since the Germans had never developed a democratic regime, they were not in a position to engender a native version of Sherlock Holmes. Their deep-founded susceptibilities to life abroad enabled them, nevertheless, to enjoy the lovely myth of the English detective.

Both Sherlock Holmes and the imitators flourished in abundance in Germany during the period 1914 to 1918, when it seemed that a detective film only needed to have either Sherlock Holmes or an imitation with the German idea of an English-sounding name to be certain of success. As the war dragged on, the film censorship appears to have prohibited the exhibition of non-German Sherlock Holmes films, but the home-made product was even turned out in various seasonal series.

The process began with *The Hound of the Baskervilles*, written by Richard Oswald, directed by Rudolph Meinert and featuring Alwin Neuss as Holmes. Conan Doyle's macabre tale of the legendary ghost-hound, roaming the moors and causing the deaths of successive members of the Baskerville family, obviously made a profound impression on Richard Oswald, for he returned to the subject in another film version years later.

The film proved to be a major stepping-stone in Oswald's film-making career. It was tremendously successful in America, and in most of Europe, either during or after the war. In Berlin in July 1914, it was honoured by a visit from the Prince August Wilhelm, Prince Friedrich Sigismund and Prince Friedrich Karl, who saw it at a cinema in the elegant Kurfurstendamm. Its success enabled the same production team to go straight on to make a sequel entitled *The Isolated House* (*The Hound of the Baskervilles – Part II*), in which the villain Stapleton, captured at the end of *The Hound*, escapes to an extraordinary submersible house that he has built in a lake. Sherlock Holmes, trapped in Baskerville Castle by Stapleton, escapes by calling for help on 'a pocket wireless outfit'! Later, when Holmes is struggling to free Lord and Lady Baskerville, who are trapped in the submerged house, Stapleton breaks the windows, allowing the water to enter, but Holmes manages to reach the mechanism and raise the house in time. Stapleton finally perishes by submerging in the house which blows up. This, it need hardly be said, was not from a Conan Doyle story.

By this time Vitascope had merged with Projections A. G. Union, under whose banner the second film appeared. Presumably as a result of a power struggle at the top, the president of the Vitascope Company, Julius Greenbaum, formed the Greenbaum-Film Company, and in 1915 there appeared Greenbaum advertisements for *The Hound of the Baskervilles – Part III* and *The Hound of the Baskervilles – Part IV*, with Alwin Neuss and the cast from Parts I and II, scenarios by Richard Oswald and this time Oswald also as director.

The reaction from Union was one of massive retaliation. They rushed into production with their own *Hound – Part III*, and rushed into print with advertisements announcing the legal action they were taking against the actors for breach of contract and against Greenbaum-Film for violation of Union's rights to the story. (It is not clear which rights they were referring to, but it seems doubtful that they really had any rights at all.) The upshot of it all was that the Greenbaum films were prohibited in Germany for the duration of the war, while the vindictive Union Company did nothing further to continue the series themselves.

Alwin Neuss moved on to the Decla (Deutsche Eclair) Company, where his first production was yet another Sherlock Holmes film, *A Scream in the Night* (1915). This was a full-blooded detection-and-action story which had Holmes operating in the USA, in a curious New York which had both Wall Street and Bond Street in it, with the climax in a hunting lodge in the Yosemite Valley. The film was directed by Neuss and written by Paul Rosenhayn, a novelist whose prodigious output at that time included scenarios for three or four different film companies as well as adaptations of his own novels for the screen. Neuss later went on to appear as a pseudo-English detective called Tom Shark in a long-running series by Decla.

Rudolph Meinert, who had directed *The Hound Parts I and II*, formed his own company, Meinert-Film, whose first film was *William Voss* (1916). The title figure, Voss, was a sort of Germanic Arsène Lupin, and, like many successful characters of this type, he later became the subject of a series. In this particular film he was up against a master detective whose name, once again, was Sherlock Holmes. Soon after this, Meinert-Film launched their own English-type detective with their Harry Higgs series.

In 1917 the Kowo Company began a new Sherlock Holmes series consisting of four films written by Paul Rosenhayn. Among his other commitments at that time Rosenhayn was writing the scenarios for the Joe Jenkins series of films, based on his own stories concerning yet another English-type detective, and the consequent breakdown in his health was hardly surprising. Kowo ran into financial troubles and had difficulty in getting their first series as far as four films. However, they managed to restore the situation and by the summer of 1918 they were proudly announcing yet another Sherlock Holmes series, this time featuring, as they claimed, 'the first ever German portrayer of Sherlock Holmes on the live stage' – Ferdinand Bonn. This series ran into 1919, and finally in 1920 Greenbaum-Film wound up the whole slightly crazy business with, believe it or not, *The Hound of the Baskervilles – Parts V and VI*!

During the period from 1910 to 1920 the cinema made a great transition from a purely novelty entertainment to an extension of the art of drama, and dramatic presentations increased in length and improved in quality. They also increased in quantity so much that material which was borrowed from books and plays was consumed very rapidly. As with Gillette and his play, many famous actors and artistes were persuaded to give performances in their best-known roles for the voracious kinematograph. Every week brought forth screen versions of old favourites and new best-sellers, and publishers scrambled to bring out reprints and new editions to coincide with the ever-increasing output of 'films of the book'.

It was not long before several film companies hit upon the idea of various extended series of films based on works by individual authors. By 1920 the Stoll Film Company of London had devised several such series of shorter films, based on short stories. One successful series was based on Sax Rohmer's stories of Dr Fu Manchu. Another series proved so popular that it ran to a second and then a third series, the whole extending over three years. These series featured Eille Norwood as Sherlock Holmes.

Apart from *The Speckled Band*, the only other dramatisation of Sherlock Holmes made by Conan Doyle himself was a one-act play entitled *The Crown Diamond*. It is a curious example of a dramatisation that was later made into a short story – a reversal of the usual process. Unfortunately the play was a very contrived and meretricious piece, and even in its subsequent form as the short story *The Adventure of the Mazarin Stone*, it is probably the least admired and most adversely criticised story of the whole Holmes saga.

Both the play and the story begin with the arrival of Dr Watson at the Baker Street rooms and his conversation with Billy the page. Billy draws aside a curtain revealing a wax dummy of Sherlock Holmes in a chair in the bow window, and then departs. There enters a tall, bent old woman in black, wearing a veil. She upsets Watson by her rudeness. 'I knew you wouldn't be Mr. Holmes,' she tells him, 'I'd always heard *he* was a handsome man.' She approaches Holmes's safe before Watson can restrain her and as she does so all the lights go out and four red lamps spring up, with the words 'DON'T TOUCH' between them. After a few seconds the lights go on and standing beside Dr Watson is Sherlock Holmes, having shed his old-woman disguise in the darkness.

Holmes is visited by two criminals whom he briefly leaves alone in the room. During his absence one of them sets off the 'DON'T TOUCH' lamps and in the brief spell of darkness Holmes changes places with the dummy, so that he can listen to their conversation and snatch the Crown Diamond from them.

Like the revival of *The Speckled Band*, this unhappy one-act episode coincided with the appearance of a series of Sherlock Holmes silent films. It was performed at the London Coliseum in May 1921, with Dennis Neilson-Terry as Sherlock Holmes. On the same variety bill, together with dancers, comedians and jugglers, were the established favourites Muriel George and Ernest Butcher in their repertoire of folk songs, and 'Walter Williams, famous revue star, with Gertrude Lawrence, from the Vaudeville Theatre, in songs and dances.' In the midst of such a programme, and amongst the cosy rattle of matinée teacups, a Sherlock Holmes stage drama must have seemed very out-of-place. Somewhat out-of-date as well, for the ominous last item on the programme was 'The latest news on the screen.'

The writing had been on the wall for some considerable time. Films were rapidly ousting live shows, and throughout the country theatres were either closing down or were installing cinematograph projectors and screens in partial or total surrender to the competition.

CHAPTER 4

Eille Norwood

Now they have been done by the Stoll Company with Eille
Norwood as Holmes, and it was worth all the extra expense
to get so fine a production.

Conan Doyle

Eille Norwood appeared as Sherlock Holmes in no fewer than forty-
seven films, a total that is now only likely to be exceeded by television
films; he capped this achievement with an extensive run in a Sherlock
Holmes stage play.

The Stoll Company's first series, *The Adventures of Sherlock Holmes*,
was made in 1921. It consisted of fifteen episodes selected at random
from the short stories. This series was directed by Maurice Elvey, and
later the same year Elvey produced a full-length version of *The Hound
of the Baskervilles*. When Elvey went to Hollywood, George Ridgewell
took over the direction of the second and third series.

The second series, made in 1922, was entitled *The Further Adventures
of Sherlock Holmes*. The fifteen episodes were again taken at random
from the short stories. The third series, *The Last Adventures of Sherlock
Holmes*, was made in 1923, also fifteen episodes. Late in 1923 Maurice
Elvey returned from America and produced the last, and most expen-
sive, of the Stoll Sherlock Holmes films – *The Sign of Four*.

This total of forty-seven films is remarkable also for the high
standards of production and performance that were maintained
throughout the series. Perhaps the finest was Maurice Elvey's *The
Hound*, an extremely well-made version which stayed close to the
original story. The film demonstrates quite clearly the sure touch that

marks all Elvey's films, even at the high rate at which they were then produced.

The previous Sherlock Holmes series by Eclair had been made prior to the Great War, when a totally different way of life existed, but Stoll set everything firmly in the 1920s – an aspect of their films that disturbed some people. 'My only criticism of the films,' wrote Conan Doyle, 'is that they introduce telephones, motor cars and other luxuries of which the Victorian Holmes never dreamed.' Of course, the Stoll Company was making no attempt to present a Victorian Holmes, and, after all, Conan Doyle's Holmes was not above using motor cars and telephones in the later stories; but the point is a valid one, for the Stoll series marked the change to a practice of presenting Sherlock Holmes in a modernised environment, a practice that continued on the cinema screen until after the Second World War.

In spite of the 1920s setting (a feature that adds an unintended attraction when the films are seen today), the Stoll films were mostly close adaptations of the original stories. Conan Doyle gave his co-operation in the making of the series and was greatly impressed by Eille Norwood's performances. He wrote of Norwood: 'He has that rare quality which can only be described as glamour, which compels you to watch an actor eagerly even when he is doing nothing.'

Eille Norwood's massive calm was quite deliberate and studied. Speaking about playing the role, he said:

My idea of Holmes is that he is absolutely quiet. Nothing ruffles him but he is a man who intuitively seizes on points without revealing that he has done so, and nurses them up with complete inaction until the moment when he is called upon to exercise his wonderful detective powers. Then he is like a cat – the person he is after is the only person in all the world, and he is oblivious of everything else till his quarry is run to earth.

Norwood fitted Doyle's own notion of Sherlock Holmes extremely well: 'He has that brooding eye which excites expectation and he has also an unrivalled power of disguise.' Norwood's talent for character make-up was put to excellent use in these films, and every opportunity was taken to introduce Sherlock Holmes in a bewildering array of disguises. It certainly helped to enliven Norwood's acting, as he was otherwise confined to a rather undemonstrative portrayal of Holmes, as is most noticeable when the Stoll films are seen today. Compared with the exaggerated gestures and grimaces of many of the supporting players, Norwood is calm to the point of stolidity. His great achievement was to give a consistently satisfying performance throughout a long series *without the benefit of dialogue*, which is essential to a complete portrayal.

After Eille Norwood had acted in these three series of Sherlock Holmes films, his success in a Sherlock Holmes stage play was almost a foregone conclusion. This was quite the opposite of the usual situation when stage performers repeated their successes on the screen, as in 1916 when Essanay had a guaranteed winner with their film of William Gillette's play.

Norwood's play was entitled *The Return of Sherlock Holmes* and was written by J. E. Harold Terry and Arthur Rose. It was presented at the Prince's Theatre, London, in 1923, after which it toured the provinces for almost a year. The plot was a mixture from four of the short stories – *The Disappearance of Lady Frances Carfax*, *The Empty House*, *Charles Augustus Milverton* and *The Red-Headed League* – but the basic story line was the same as Gillette's play *Sherlock Holmes*, even down to the sensational escape from the gang's underground hideout.

The play was filled with action and positively crammed with characters. 'The most striking feature of the piece, after Mr. Norwood's effective performance in the title part, is the multiplicity of criminals to whom he is opposed all at once,' wrote *The Times* critic, adding that 'for once it is not hampered by an overstressed love theme'.

In place of Alice Faulkner in the hands of the Larrabees, there is Lady Frances Carfax who is being swindled by the villainous Schlessingers, and being slowly poisoned by them into the bargain. Thwarted by Sherlock Holmes, the Schlessingers appeal for help to Colonel Moran, who is already straining to avenge the death of his former chief, Professor Moriarty.

Eille Norwood's mastery of make-up was not overlooked. In the play Holmes disguises himself as Colonel Moran's German servant, and succeeds in locating the gang. He frees Lady Carfax's fiancé and escapes from the gang, in a near replica of Gillette's Gas Chamber scene. After shooting across Baker Street from the Empty House and failing to kill Holmes, Colonel Moran is finally decoyed by the wax

Page 51 (above) Gillette's
famous Gas Chamber scene
reproduced exactly for the
screen in *Sherlock Holmes*
(Goldwyn, 1922), John Barrymore as Holmes; (*left*) Dr
Watson (H. G. Stoker) is
warned off the window by
Holmes (Eille Norwood) in the
stage play *The Return of
Sherlock Holmes* (1923)

Page 52 (*above*) Colonel Gore-King of Scotland Yard (Alan Mowbray), Sherlock Holmes (Clive Brook) and the insufferable Billy (Howard Leeds) in *Sherlock Holmes* (Fox, 1932). Billy, in his all-American messenger-boy outfit, is holding Holmes's portable detective kit; (*below*) Sherlock Holmes (Arthur Wontner), Dr Watson (Ian Fleming) and Lady Violet Lumsden (Jane Welsh) in *The Missing Rembrandt* (Twickenham, 1932)

dummy of Holmes and captured in the Baker Street rooms. Indeed, it was quite a lot like 'The Return of William Gillette's Sherlock Holmes'.

The Stage commented:

Mr. Norwood, playing throughout with finesse, imperturbable cynicism, and quiet force, carried off the honours of the evening on Tuesday with his admirable acting, as well as his skilful production work . . . Warm credit is due also to the deft adapters of the later stories, and to them Sir Arthur Conan Doyle, at the end of the performance, paid a deserving tribute, saying 'I am but the grandpapa; these,' pointing to Mr. Terry and Mr. Rose, 'are the parents.'

The drama critic of *The Daily Telegraph* celebrated the opening night with a review of a somewhat heady brew:

Wherein lies the perfect exquisiteness of this play? What is the quality in it which compels an audience so vast as that of last night to hang upon it in a fascinated silence 'like birds the charming serpent draws'? The more we ask ourselves this question the more convinced we become that its irresistibleness lies in the fact that, from end to end, there is not a character in it who is not a fully-qualified candidate for a lunatic asylum. Some are preternaturally acute, others preternaturally wicked, others again preternaturally foolish, but . . . all, all are preternaturally mad. And the more seriously they take themselves and their preposterous doings the more delightful they become to your true playgoer, who – bless you! – goes to the theatre not for fact, but for fantasy; not for reality, which is one thing, but for 'realism' which is another and very different matter.

The review concluded: 'Mr. Eille Norwood moves grandly and gloomily through the part of Holmes, and is wildly applauded at the end of each act.'

That phrase seems to sum up how Eille Norwood impersonated Sherlock Holmes, 'grandly and gloomily'.

In 1922 Sam Goldwyn launched the Great Profile John Barrymore as the Great Profile Sherlock Holmes. At that time the only Sherlock Holmes film rights not held by Stoll, then making their series of two-reelers with Norwood, were the rights to the Gillette play, and Goldwyn snapped them up. Casting Barrymore as Holmes was a shrewd move, for he was immensely popular in those days and he had what many impersonators have lacked – impressive features for the role. Unfortunately, Barrymore was not very tall, so the remainder of the cast had to be very carefully selected so as not to overshadow the star.

The film, entitled *Sherlock Holmes*, was issued in Britain as *Moriarty*, presumably to avoid clashing too obviously with the Stoll series. Moriarty was played by a well-known silent film villain of the period – Gustav von Seyffertitz, who was made to appear a grotesque bogeyman rather than a menacing Napoleon of crime. His costume was almost Dickensian, with a stove-pipe hat and an Abbé Liszt hairstyle. Albert Parker, the film's director, maintains that von Seyffertitz did not overdo or caricature the part; in that case he was clearly working under a handicap. (At one point in the film Holmes disguised himself as Moriarty, which must have given Barrymore a field day in the make-up department.)

The plot of the film followed the Gillette play, with a specially written prologue showing Holmes and Watson as 'college mates at Cambridge'. Exteriors for this part of the film were shot at St John's College. A number of locations in London were also used, including the Albert Embankment, parts of Stepney, and Lambeth Pier. Since Baker Street itself was not really suitable, even in 1921, the then-attractive frontages of Torrington Square were used for Baker Street exteriors.

Hampton Court was the setting for a scene involving a houseboat. As the director Albert Parker admitted: 'There was no such episode in Gillette's play, nor in the *Adventures* as far as I am aware. A houseboat struck us, however, as a picturesque location, and a novel one so far as American films are concerned, so we decided on this as the scene of a murder which Holmes investigates in our version.'

The cast was filled with interesting names such as the ubiquitous Hedda Hopper (as Madge Larrabee), Reginald Denny, Louis Wolheim and William H. Powell, who subsequently became a screen detective himself, first as Philo Vance and later as Nick Charles in *The Thin Man* series. A team of actors to gladden the heart of any director. But that was far outweighed by the trouble Albert Parker had with his star:

> I came over to England after Barrymore had arrived, and I was told that Barrymore couldn't be seen or found anywhere. I finally tracked him down to a tiny little attic room at the Ritz Hotel, and I went in and there was

Barrymore sitting up in bed blind drunk. The room was in a terrible state. There were even gin bottles in his shoes!

Eventually I got him to work, and I can tell you I had a pretty rough time with him on location in England. We had rows; it was a very tricky time. We went to Switzerland on location; more rows. They loaned us a whole train for filming, and even shifted a whole load of snow on one of the mountain tops when we got to the top and found there wasn't any! It was all done with great difficulty, as Barrymore was drunk most of the time.

We returned to the States when we had all the location shots, and then I really had it out with Barrymore, a *real* row. I told him he was killing himself, and so forth. I really let him have it. And Barrymore must have seen the strength of what I was saying, and you know, he never touched a drop while we were filming all the interior scenes. I did it because I was fond of Barrymore, and I think he gave a very good, restrained performance in those scenes.

We had rows over the leading lady too. Barrymore objected to her a lot. He didn't like any women. We reached the point where we had one scene left to take, and Barrymore said – I'm not going to do another shot with that woman again – and he walked off the set, and I didn't know what I was going to do. I got the idea that we could just show her shadow in the cab, and then Barrymore had to run out and jump on the hansom cab. I had got to cajole Barrymore to do the shot, so I sent Carol Dempster home. But I put her coloured maid inside the cab, where she would be hidden from Jack Barrymore, so he wouldn't know. I set the cameras up and then went to Barrymore and said – O.K. We're ready – and he said – I told you, I'm not going to – and I said – you don't have to, Jack. It's all right. There's the cab. You have to run on the sidewalk and get on the cab. Then talk with your hands. Well, it was one of the highlights of the film. He got there and he got such a shock when he saw the maid in the cab, but he did a marvellous bit of ad-libbing. It was great.

The film got marvellous reviews, you know. It broke records in New York. It was my favourite picture that I made. After that film Jack and I became great friends. I was very fond of him, and I think he was fond of me. But he was absolutely crazy, mad as a hatter, not good for himself at any time, but lovable.

Dr Watson in the film was Roland Young, and John Barrymore has left a comment on Young's performance expressed in typical Barrymore fashion:

When the modest, self-effacing Roland appeared on my horizon, I took a great liking to him; so much so that I began to feel sorry for him during our scenes together. For once in my life, I decided to be somewhat decent towards a colleague. I suggested a little stage business now and then, so that such a charming, agreeable thespian might not be altogether lost in the shuffle. When I saw the completed film, I was flabbergasted, stunned, and almost became an atheist on the spot. That quiet, agreeable bastard had stolen, not one, but every damned scene! This consummate artist and myself have been close friends for years, but I wouldn't think of trusting him on any stage. He is such a splendid gentleman in real life, but what a cunning, larcenous demon when on the boards!

At the time that talking pictures arrived, most of the silent feature films in production were suddenly out-of-date. Some were remade, or had sound added. Many were either scrapped or they were released and promptly ignored by the fickle public.

Among these casualties of the march of progress was the last silent Sherlock Holmes film, *Der Hund von Baskerville*, made in Berlin in 1929 with a cast of mixed nationalities. The English actress Alma Taylor was cast with Americans Betty Bird and Carlyle Blackwell, while the remainder of the cast appears to have been German, Italian and Russian. Carlyle Blackwell, who played Sherlock Holmes, had been one of the busiest American film actors of the decade 1910 to 1920, after which he worked in Europe. Then came the talkies and, as with many silent stars, his career was as good as over. His features were quite reasonable for the role, and although the adaptation was set in the twenties, he was equipped with a deerstalker – probably the only time in any continental Sherlock Holmes film.

The director, Richard Oswald, had an understandable affection for the story, for he had written the scenario for the first film version of *The Hound* in 1914, and it had proved a turning point in his career. He directed a number of sequels, and had rapidly become one of the leading film producers and directors in Germany. Apart from his fondness for *The Hound*, the story was, then and later, very popular in Germany, and Oswald's 1929 version of the tale displayed the moody settings, heavily dramatic lighting and firm direction that were characteristic of his talent.

As for Sherlock Holmes, *Der Kinematograph* had the following to say: 'Since the incidents take place in England, and since Sherlock Holmes was always portrayed by his creator as an Englishman, we have in this film one of the best-known Anglo Saxon film players

(C. Blackwell), but for our taste he is not the ideal embodiment of the shrewd secret policeman.'

That comment seems to summarise the way that the Germans like and admire Sherlock Holmes as an Anglo Saxon character, and fail to understand him as anything but a secret policeman.

Silent Sherlock Holmes films may seem rather quaint and amusing today, but at the time they were made many of them were very good films, and one or two can still be regarded as first-class. Taken simply as crime and adventure films, they were exciting enough, and almost the only Holmesian thing about some of them was the name of the principal character. Apart from that, they followed the usual formulae – mistaken identity, accidental detection, surprise, and lots and lots of pursuits. Needless to say, there was neither real detection nor deduction by Holmes. Later, when film rights were sold, a closer resemblance to the stories was required, although the emphasis was still very much on dramatic action. It was not until sound films were introduced that it became possible for Holmes to deduce and detect without seriously holding up the action; a possibility that was not always brought about.

Basil Mitchell's play *The Holmeses of Baker Street*, which appeared in 1933, was not only the most original and amusing dramatisation of Sherlock Holmes to be staged; it was also a gentle tilt at the highly successful play *The Barretts of Wimpole Street*, produced two or three years previously, which had shown the agonising struggles of Elizabeth Barrett to marry Robert Browning, despite all the obstacles and objections raised by her monstrously overbearing father.

The theme of the domineering father attempting to browbeat his rebellious daughter was imitated by Basil Mitchell, but was neatly turned so that instead of forbidding marriage the father actively encourages it.

Set in the years of Sherlock Holmes's retirement, the story presented Holmes as a widower, living in the country with his daughter Shirley, and interested only in beekeeping. During a brief visit to their Baker Street flat they become involved with the latest outrage of the notorious White X gang – the projected theft of a celebrated Black Pearl, audaciously announced in advance.

Shirley Holmes is highly excited at the prospect of being able to employ the deductive powers she has so clearly inherited, but her father forbids any participation. He explains to Watson, who is visiting them at the flat, that his own acute powers of observation and deduction had been the cause of an unhappy marriage for him, culminating in the premature death of his wife. Holmes is therefore determined that the same thing shall not happen with Shirley, and is anxious that she shall soon become married and domesticated. Even Mr Canning (the young man who keeps the wireless shop downstairs), in whom she seems interested, would do.

Of course, Shirley has other ideas and, in collaboration with Mrs Watson, she fakes the theft of her father's new queen bee in order to keep him in London, but during the night the queen bee is really stolen.

Inspector Withers of Scotland Yard calls on Sherlock Holmes, requesting his assistance in preventing the White X gang's theft, but Holmes is adamant in his refusal to resume criminal detection, and eventually he and Shirley return to their country home, taking with them the Watsons and Mr Canning, all of whom have been invited for the weekend.

Shirley is certain that her father would never have left London unless he had recovered his queen bee, and by now she has convinced herself that the Black Pearl has been sent to Holmes for safe keeping, hidden in the queen-bee cage. Although Shirley and Canning become engaged, Shirley's observations and deductions lead her to the uncomfortable suspicion that Canning is implicated in the activities of the White X gang, and in the dénouement she is mortified to see her conclusions borne out by the facts. But at the last minute Sherlock Holmes, observing her distress, comes to their assistance and clears the young man from the case. The play ends with Holmes commenting happily to Watson that Shirley's feminine instincts will soon overcome her intellectual powers and all will be well.

The construction and dialogue of the piece had been carried out beautifully by Basil Mitchell, and the majority of the Press gave the London production a very warm reception. In *The Daily Telegraph*, W. A. Darlington began his review with great enthusiasm – '*The Holmeses of Baker Street*, by Basil Mitchell, is thundering good entertainment'; and *The Morning Post* stated that 'This is the best Sherlock Holmes play there has yet been . . . It was received last night with unreserved and universal applause.'

Great praise was given to Felix Aylmer's sensitive portrayal of Sherlock Holmes. *The Times* wrote:

> At the very end there is a twist of sentiment which, because Miss Rosemary Ames's Shirley has not won us to it, jars a little, but for nine-tenths of its course the story is an admirable one with just the smooth excitement that one expects of a Holmes adventure and decorations of humour that are not only verbally ingenious but accord naturally with what is already known and what Mr. Mitchell now tells us of Holmes's character . . . But it is Mr. Felix Aylmer who makes the evening's success, as if he were playing in a masterpiece, avoiding melodrama, rigidly avoiding burlesque, giving to the whole adventure precisely the right balance of seriousness and amusement. As a study of detail, a light essay in interpretation, and an entertainment it is a flawless piece of acting.

In the light of such a welcome it is very hard to understand the play's failure. It ran at the Lyric Theatre for only ten days, followed by two weeks at minor London theatres. Felix Aylmer certainly enjoyed performing in the play, and offered an explanation:

> *The Holmeses of Baker Street* was great fun to do. It is always disappointing when a play fails, and I certainly attributed the collapse to the line taken by some of the critics. I am fairly certain that James Agate came out with the general proposition that no author should steal a character made famous by another, and that it was the duty of critics to come down hard on such a flagrant case. Audiences probably take a different line but, hearing that a Sherlock Holmes play was offered, before going to see it would want to know which story had been chosen, and when they heard that it was a new one and not by Conan Doyle at all, would be likely to hang fire. We might have picked up, but didn't run long enough to find out.
>
> As well as I remember, the suspense quality, on which such plays largely depend, may have been damaged by Nigel Playfair's treatment of Watson as essentially a comic character. In some way the dramatic climax, with the arrest, missed fire . . . The author's view of the production? I never had it from him myself, but I fancy he would support my impression that we fell between two stools, sometimes poking fun at the Sherlock Holmes legend, and then asking to be taken seriously.

Another factor which almost certainly contributed to the early closing of the play was the poor reception given to the actress (Rosemary Ames) who portrayed Shirley Holmes, and who happened to be the wife of the impresario concerned – B. A. Meyer. James Agate did not even condescend to mention her name in his savage review: 'The young lady who played the heroine is presumably proposing to adopt the stage as a profession, and it must be said once again that it is a great disservice to give a leading part to any young player whose proficiency hardly extends to a minor role.'

CHAPTER 5

The Return of Sherlock Holmes

Two solid external factors that have contributed to the un-
equalled fame of Holmes are the illustrations and the numerous
stage and screen plays made from the stories.

Howard Haycraft

Various films are claimed to be the first talking picture; some were really silents with sound effects and portions of dialogue added; others were part-talking and part-musical background, and so on. But in the area of Sherlock Holmes films there is no dispute.

It was Clive Brook who made history in a small way by appearing in the first Sherlock Holmes sound film. All-talking, all-deducing, as it were. Perhaps that was one of the troubles with the film, for the advent of talkies had necessitated cumbersome sound-proofing round the cameras, and overnight the movies had become static. 'Canned theatre' was a fashionable term of derision of the time.

Already a matinée idol, Clive Brook was no newcomer to the movies, having made his first film in England in 1921. He soon joined the procession of British actors making their way to Hollywood, and in 1929 he starred for Paramount in *The Return of Sherlock Holmes*. Clive Brook described some of the background to the film:

David Selznick was the head of production at Paramount in those days, and he put me in a number of films, and then one day he said – I've got something I think you'd do awfully well – and it was this Sherlock Holmes film. He said I looked like him, you see, and that's why we made it. A lot of the reviews said I'm very much like Sherlock Holmes. I can't see that at all. Still, as long as they think so . . .

I was on my way back to America in the Olympic when I got a cable telling me that *The Return of Sherlock Holmes* was to be the next film I was to make. It was made in Paramount's Astoria Studio in New York, and on board a liner.

We had a lot of trouble during the shooting of the film. The director's work had hitherto been confined to the theatre, and he had little experience of movies, and how they are made; and he was misguided enough to try to teach the studio personnel their job. He insisted on having four-sided sets constructed, to assist the actors in a feeling of reality, not understanding that cameramen and sound-recordists could not operate in such a set-up. Finally, he left before the picture was completed and I finished directing the film myself.

Nevertheless, I very much enjoyed Holmes. I characterized him larger than life and this permitted much comedy. The versions of Sherlock Holmes I've seen seem inclined to make him a clever solver of crimes but gave little to his foibles and eccentricities. As far as I am concerned Conan Doyle in his stories certainly made Holmes larger than life; and that's how I played it.

Using an ocean liner as the setting for the film limited the number of sets required, and virtually eliminated exterior and location scenes; both were important advantages in the first awkward years of sound film making.

The regular principal characters are all on the liner because Dr Watson's daughter, Mary, has lost her boy-friend Roger Longmore. Roger has been abducted while trying to trace the murderer of his father. Certain clues lead Holmes to dash off to Cherbourg to catch the liner for America, accompanied by Watson and Mary. On board the liner Holmes disguises himself as a member of the ship's orchestra (violinist, of course), and he later switches to the disguise of a cabin steward, which gives him access to the boots and shoes of his suspects. By painting the soles with phosphorous, he finds a trail to the cabin of Professor Moriarty and the cabin where Roger is held captive. Holmes proceeds to wire up Moriarty's cabin with that of the ship's captain, and then allows himself to be discovered on board by Moriarty who boldly invites him to supper. Eventually Moriarty believes that he has caught Holmes with a poisoned thorn fixed in a cigarette case, and boasts to his dying victim of his criminal achievements. Thanks to the hook-up between cabins he has been heard by Watson and the captain, and, realising the game is up he takes his own poison.

The strong and convincing acting of Clive Brook and Harry T. Morey (Moriarty) appear to have carried the rather preposterous story which, according to Basil Dean, was not allowed to be based on any of Conan Doyle's tales, Paramount having paid $5,000 just to use Holmes and Watson. Nevertheless, the film was successful and reviews were generous with praise for Clive Brook's polished entertaining performance and his versatility as a character actor.

Paramount were also having a success with two series of films featuring Philo Vance, the dilettante American private detective, played by William Powell, and Dr Fu Manchu, played by Warner Oland, and in August 1929 the go-ahead David Selznick wrote to one of his colleagues: 'I wonder if it would not be entertaining to have a little burlesque in the Revue of Philo Vance and Sherlock Holmes in pursuit of Fu Manchu . . . a skit about these three celebrated characters of fiction, and of Paramount Pictures, might be intriguing and diverting.'

The revue, *Paramount on Parade*, was one of a number of filmed extravaganzas presented by the major studios at the beginning of the talkies to show off all the talent they had under contract. Selznick's idea was adopted, and the sketch, *Murder Will Out*, duly appeared, although Paramount never made another Sherlock Holmes film.

The talkies brought with them a spate of remakes of successful films, especially film versions of the classics, and of course the Holmes stories were no exception. Once Clive Brook had blazed the trail, the screens of Europe and America seemed to be flooded with Sherlock Holmes films, with as many as five appearing in one year (1932).

First in time after Clive Brook was Arthur Wontner, who is discussed later in this chapter, closely followed by Raymond Massey in *The Speckled Band*. This 1931 version had Lyn Harding in his original stage role of Dr Grimesby Rylott. Doyle's story line was followed to a certain extent, although the settings were modernised, with stenographers and filing cabinets in the Baker Street rooms! Lyn Harding kept his unsubtle melodramatic style of acting unchanged for the screen, while the Holmes of Raymond Massey was counted a good try.

The Hound of the Baskervilles, with additional dialogue by Edgar Wallace, sounds like the poor relation of that famous Hollywood screen credit 'A Midsummer Night's Dream by William Shakespeare, with additional dialogue by Sam Taylor.' Unfortunately, this 1932 *Hound* is lost, so we are unable to assess Edgar Wallace's contribution, but the film appears to have been undistinguished. The production was described in a nine-week series of articles in the British magazine *Film Weekly*, the readers of which had voted *The Hound* as the story they most wished to be filmed. Whether they wished it to be set in 1932 England was never made clear.

Also set in the same period was Clive Brook's second feature film as Sherlock Holmes.

'That was a terrible film,' said Mr. Brook. 'It was made by Fox. I was under a long-term contract with Paramount and they loaned me to Fox. The studios used to do very well out of loaning us actors to other studios for large sums of money. We were under contract and were just paid the same salary anyway.

'So Fox asked Paramount for me for a Holmes film and I foolishly thought – Sherlock Holmes, fine! I'll do it – and I didn't have a script, which was unusual for me. I usually read a first copy of the script to see what I was doing. I got on to the set and began reading this thing and I discovered that it was ghastly from my point of view, bringing it up to date with gangsters from America, and Holmes engaged to that girl . . .'

'That girl' was Alice Faulkner, and the film purported to be based on the William Gillette play, but her name was the only slender connection. As played by Miriam Jordan, Alice was a charming product of the English upper classes, engaged to Sherlock Holmes who is about to retire to a life of chicken-farming, since his life's work is over and Moriarty is sentenced. But Moriarty escapes in a truly American style gaol-break, and sets out to wreak his vengeance. He convenes a summit conference of leading criminals from Europe and America, and organises a crime wave designed to bring discredit and death to Sherlock Holmes and Colonel Gore-King of Scotland Yard (Alan Mowbray). Behind this smokescreen, Moriarty also organises a spectacular robbery of the Faulkner bank (owned by Alice's father), with Alice and Billy, the page-boy, held as hostages. One could easily wish that only Alice was rescued by Holmes at the climax, for the Billy in this film was quite insufferable. Performed by an American youngster who was incapable either of imitating a Cockney voice or indeed of acting at all, Billy was used throughout the film as a substitute for Watson, with even the closing line of the picture being 'Elementary, my dear Billy.' In fact Watson was very nearly written out of the film altogether, and served no purpose by his presence, appearing only in two scenes, and having absurd lines like 'Great heavens, Holmes! It is positively an ambuscade!' Billy, on the other hand, was built up in importance and made the listening block for Holmes's observations and deductions. Many of these changes were made while the film was in progress, which was unsettling for the actors, especially Clive Brook:

> I didn't like making it very much at all. The American director (William K. Howard) lacked any respect for Conan Doyle's characters, and ruthlessly introduced anything that he thought would be attractive at the box office. Nor had he any respect for the script, since he extemporised new scenes as he went along, with no consideration for the actors who had no time in which to learn new lines.

This was most unfortunate, because the movie turned out to be a zestful, rapidly paced detective film and for 1932 was very good. It was just not the right approach for a Sherlock Holmes film, but in spite of William K. Howard's obvious intention to make a slick, American-style crime story, Clive Brook still managed to convey the polish and humour that had been such a feature of his previous Holmes film.

Surely only the Hollywood of those days would think of taking the actor who was Clive Brook's Watson and featuring him as Sherlock Holmes less than a year later! Such was Reginald Owen's unique distinction, in *A Study in Scarlet*, another well-made vigorous detective film that bore no resemblance whatever to Conan Doyle's novel of that title. Based on Agatha Christie's *Ten Little Niggers* would have been a rather better guide.

But overshadowing all other portrayers of the role in the 1930s was an impersonator of Sherlock Holmes whose appearance and performance made the rest seem like burlesque. 'No other Sherlock Holmes is genuine – accept no substitute,' wrote an American film critic, alluding to Arthur Wontner.

As a leading British actor, Arthur Wontner had played several detective roles on the stage during the 1920s:

In those days my thoughts had often wandered to the *doyen* of fictional detectives, Sherlock Holmes. People had remarked so frequently: 'You really ought to play Sherlock Holmes. I've never seen anyone so like Sidney Paget's drawings.' I had met Conan Doyle a year or so previously and we had talked about his stories, discussing whether he would dramatise one for me.

We did not think of films, which in those days, and in England at any rate, were nothing like they are now. I was overjoyed when the famous author said he would like me to play his celebrated sleuth. But the stage production did not mature.

In September 1930, Wontner played the title role in Donald Stuart's stage play *Sexton Blake* and a number of reviewers remarked on Wontner's striking resemblance to the generally accepted appearance of Sherlock Holmes. From that time the notion took shape and in December of that year he had a screen test at Twickenham Film Productions and was cast by Julius Hagen to play Sherlock Holmes in *The Sleeping Cardinal*, the first of what became a series of five films.

Money was not plentiful during the making of the Wontner films, with one exception. Yet the atmosphere of these films was very convincing, with very little perceptible artificiality. This was partly due to Arthur Wontner himself, who was keenly interested in the character of Sherlock Holmes and wrote much of his own dialogue, frequently incorporating little passages from the stories.

The Sleeping Cardinal ran for over a month on Broadway – an unprecedented achievement for a British film in 1931. The plot, based on the story *The Empty House* with incidents from *The Final Problem*, dealt with a subtle method of bank robbery by the substitution of forged banknotes for those stolen. To delay discovery further, the stolen money is to be taken abroad by the Hon Ronald Adair, whose diplomatic immunity facilitates smuggling. Moriarty, speaking from behind a portrait of a Sleeping Cardinal, threatens Adair with exposure of his card-cheating if he does not agree to this. Holmes traces the details of the robbery and its connection with both Moriarty and Adair. Adair decides against the smuggling, and is found shot. Holmes again detects the hand of Moriarty in the crime. Moriarty himself attempts to shoot Holmes from the Empty House, and is seized and taken to 221B, where he is unmasked as a family friend of the Adairs.

The naturalness and realism of the production were especially noteworthy. For instance, when Moriarty opened the window to fire across Baker Street, one heard the subdued noise of traffic and a convincing background sound atmosphere. Commonplace stuff in these days of multichannel stereophonic sound-tracks, but in 1931 exceptional.

The opening sequence of the film showed the murder of a night-watchman in the course of the bank robbery, and all that was seen on the screen was a square of moonlight cast on the floor by an unseen window, and the legs of the watchman and his assailant crossing and recrossing in their struggle. *The New York Herald Tribune* described it as 'An action expressed exclusively by sound – shuffling feet, stifled cries, a heavy strained silence and then the dying gasps of the victim tell the grisly happenings more poignantly than the full scene enacted before the eye could possibly have done.'

Arthur Wontner recalled some of the circumstances at Twickenham:

The studio wasn't much more than a big tin shed, really; not like film studios today. We used to start filming early in the morning, and continued until pretty late at night, with very few breaks. Of course, we had to stop shooting quite often when a train went by, because of the noise. But we couldn't afford much time for re-takes, and there were no elaborate re-hearsals or anything like that.

Ian Fleming's Dr Watson was a terribly well-bred gentleman, a trifle fatuous but mainly unobtrusive, but then the character of Watson should not obtrude, and Mr Fleming's self-effacement was well accomplished.

Arthur Wontner's performance as Holmes was magnificent. Here at last, we felt, was Sherlock Holmes, come to life before our eyes; the type of Holmes described by Watson in many of the stories. Arthur Wontner adopted the 'half-humorous, half-cynical vein which was his habitual attitude to those about him', and presented a cultured and gentlemanly Holmes, with 'a remarkable gentleness and courtesy in his dealings with women'. He made the character seem very natural by the 'quietly genial fashion' in which he adopted the mannerisms of the great detective. The words are Watson's, and they fit Arthur Wontner beautifully.

Praise was showered on both Wontner's performance and the film generally, in America and the colonies, as well as in Great Britain. One American reviewer, using its American title, wrote:

> I think that *Sherlock Holmes' Fatal Hour*, in addition to containing one of the smartest and most effortless performances I have ever seen, is one of the best of the English films to be shown on this side of the Atlantic. More than this, it is charged with deep suspense and excitement, and it is largely due to the poised and intelligent efforts of Mr. Wontner that this is so.

Another critic wrote, '*Sherlock Holmes' Fatal Hour* is so smooth, so beautifully timed and acted, that there is nothing to criticise adversely.' The film won the New York critics' Cinema Prize as the season's best mystery drama. This wonderful American reception took place during the time that William Gillette was covering the USA in his farewell tour as Sherlock Holmes.

Regrettably the big American success of this film did not benefit its English makers, for Warner Brothers, who distributed the film in the United Kingdom, had not even considered it worth handling in America, with the result that the American distribution rights had been sold outright to a small subsidiary company of Warners for the sum of £800.

The Sleeping Cardinal was followed almost immediately by *The Missing Rembrandt* which was based on Conan Doyle's short story *Charles Augustus Milverton*. The activities of Milverton, the blackmailer, were expanded to suit a feature-length film, with a stolen Rembrandt and an opium-den scene thrown in for good measure. Again the careful steady methods and modest formula paid off. But the success of Arthur Wontner as Sherlock Holmes had already been noticed in quarters where the exploitation of successful films spelt big business. Before filming had even begun on *The Missing Rembrandt*, Arthur Wontner had been contracted to appear next in *The Sign of Four* for Associated Radio Pictures, and immediately *The Missing Rembrandt* was completed, he moved to the new Ealing Studios to play Sherlock Holmes for the third time.

The manner in which the filming of *The Sign of Four* was undertaken is indicated by the attitude of its American producer:

> Sherlock Holmes is to be a vivid hero, a tiger among men, a fighting detec-

Page 69 (above) Holmes and Watson (Hans Albers and Heinz Ruhmann) enjoying Watson's infallible prescription in *Der Mann, der Sherlock Holmes war* (Ufa, 1937); *(below)* the most famous Holmes and Watson team of all, Basil Rathbone and Nigel Bruce, with Ida Lupino in *The Adventures of Sherlock Holmes* (Twentieth Century-Fox, 1939)

Page 70 (*above*) In their later series of films, Basil Rathbone was frequently extricating Nigel Bruce from uncomfortable situations like this from *House of Fear* (Universal, 1945); (*below*) and like this from *Woman in Green* (Universal, (1945)

tive, superhuman in every way. That is exactly what he was intended to be. You can take it from me that I am right. He lives to-day as a character slandered by those who have failed to appreciate the real man. Read about him as I have done. Was the mighty Sherlock Holmes a man who simply played the violin and drugged himself when seeking inspiration? Not a bit of it. He was a MAN! Humorous – what a sense of comedy; strong – look how he fought the great Moriarty; athletic – remember how he ran after the Hound of the Baskervilles. What a MAN! Sherlock Holmes has been pressed like a rose-leaf in a book. Now I am going to make him the man he was . . . not the dreamy detective who spent his life back-chatting with Watson.

This approach to the subject by Rowland V. Lee certainly produced a lively film of crime and detection. *The Sign of Four* bore a fair resemblance to the original novel, but the treatment of Sherlock Holmes was somewhat as described above, and Arthur Wontner was obliged to wear a tweed hat and an ankle-length greatcoat similar to those foisted on Clive Brook. In the role of Dr Watson, Ian Fleming was replaced by Ian Hunter as being more suitable for the numerous romantic sequences between Watson and Mary Morstan, for it was in the book *The Sign of Four* that Watson met and wooed Miss Morstan, who subsequently became Mrs Watson. Strange to relate, certain critics protested very indignantly about this introduction of love interest into a Sherlock Holmes film.

Arthur Wontner's fourth film appearance as Holmes was in *The Triumph of Sherlock Holmes*, which was made by Real Art Productions Ltd. This was simply Julius Hagen's Twickenham team under another name, and their capable workmanship soon erased the memory of *The Sign of Four*. Indeed, throughout the 1930s Julius Hagen exerted quite an influence generally on the quality of British films, through the high standard of the Twickenham productions. *The Triumph of Sherlock Holmes* had been planned and made under the title of Doyle's novel *The Valley of Fear*, and the name was altered just before the film was issued.

One of the main deviations from the novel was that the film opened with Sherlock Holmes actually retiring from Baker Street to his bee farm, and expressing regret that he should be doing so while Moriarty was still at large. As he is removing from Baker Street he is visited by Moriarty, and the famous interview between the two men takes place, exactly as in the story *The Final Problem*. The film makers may have overlooked what they had already done in *The Sleeping Cardinal* four years earlier, for the same interview, almost identical in dialogue and action, takes place in both films. On the other hand they may well have decided that the confrontation scene was too good not to use again!

The story included considerable flashback sequences of episodes in America depicting the lawlessness of the society called the Scowrers (Doyle's version of the infamous Molly Maguires). Birdie Edwards, the Pinkerton man who has brought about the downfall of the Scowrers, has come to England to live under the name of John Douglas. His trail is followed by Ted Balding, one of the Scowrers who has got out of prison and is intent on revenge. In the inevitable struggle between the two men Balding is killed, and to put other possible pursuers off the track, Douglas disguises the body as his own and goes into hiding,

Holmes goes to investigate and soon finds Douglas in hiding. Up to this point the film followed the novel fairly well. Then Professor Moriarty hastens to Birlstone Manor to assist Balding to escape, and finds Holmes, Watson, John Douglas and Inspector Lestrade all waiting for him. He flees up the staircase of a ruined tower and a shot from Holmes's pistol sends him toppling to what certainly appears to be his death (yet two years later he was back again, with Sherlock Holmes crossing his path and incommoding him, in *Silver Blaze*).

The Moriarty on this occasion was Lyn Harding. As Dr Grimesby Rylott in the original and subsequent stage productions of *The Speckled Band*, Harding had scored an exceptional success. But as the years went by he was left rather high and dry by the changes in drama and acting styles, and by 1935 his melodramatic declamation contrasted unfavourably with Arthur Wontner's calm and studied underplaying. He was saddled with that ridiculous scarf which first appeared round the neck of the first stage Moriarty in William Gillette's play, and his acting was of the same vintage. The Moriarty he portrayed was hardly an intellectual Napoleon of crime, but he was jolly good entertainment.

Harding repeated his portrayal of Moriarty in much the same manner in *Silver Blaze*, Arthur Wontner's fifth and final Sherlock Holmes film. This dealt with Moriarty's efforts to prevent the racehorse Silver Blaze from running. Silver Blaze disappears, and is traced by Holmes who arranges the return of the horse to the course on the day of the race. Moriarty discovers that Silver Blaze will be running, and sends Moran to the race. When the horse is a few yards from the winning post, Moran shoots it with a special silent air-gun disguised as a cine-camera. Holmes sets Watson to trail one of the criminals and this trail leads to Moriarty, whose men capture Watson. Holmes and Lestrade arrive just in time to prevent Watson being cast down a lift shaft.

During the first run of this film in London, a Friday evening performance was ragged by the audience, and the film was withdrawn from the programme for two days. 'The ragging began when some people dropped in after a good dinner and began to laugh in the wrong places,' reported the cinema manager, 'and before long others joined in the fun.' The reaction of the Press was immediate and emphatic. *The Times* boomed indignantly: 'It is to be hoped that the audiences at the Regal will for the remainder of the week comport themselves with more respect when in the presence of the great man.' *The Yorkshire Evening Post* reported that '. . . in the dress circle some self-opinionated nitwits regarded it as something beneath their dignity'. 'Nothing less than sacrilege,' spluttered *The Bystander*, 'pretty bad form . . . a miserable generation is growing up which appears to have no reverence for the immortal Sherlock Holmes.' When the film was restored to the programme nothing untoward occurred, and this seemed to emphasise the oddity of the behaviour of that Friday-night audience, who were well and truly castigated by all sections of the Press.

Nevertheless, this incident has some significance. With hindsight it clearly would not have been wise to have made any more of the Wontner series of Sherlock Holmes films in the same form.

The age of the gifted amateur detective of fiction had ended, like so many aspects of Victorian life, with the changes in society wrought by the Great War. The clever solvers of puzzles gave way to the heroes of crime and mystery adventures, the police inspectors and the agents who came in from, or stayed out in, the cold. The amateur detective could no longer function plausibly in the altered environment, and had become an anachronism. Sherlock Holmes set in the 1930s was out of place, for his type and style of detection is based on a totally different era. It was largely the portrayal by Arthur Wontner that sustained the acceptance of this situation.

When *Silver Blaze* was made, Arthur Wontner was sixty-two, and looked to be in his late forties, although his voice rather gave him away. During the Second World War he played Sherlock Holmes once more in a BBC radio version of the short story *The Boscombe Valley Mystery*. His performances as Holmes set a standard against which all subsequent portrayals can be measured. In 1933 the American author Vincent Starrett wrote 'The great Sherlock Holmes picture has not as yet been made . . . But Mr. Arthur Wontner is still available. Will not someone send a special, fast steamer for Mr. Arthur Wontner?'

'Vincent Starrett?' Arthur Wontner used to say. 'Wasn't he the American who said won't someone send a steamer for me? Well, they never did, you know, they never did.'

From the failure of the Germans to understand Sherlock Holmes as a private detective, it follows that they also failed to realise that he is essentially a creature of the 1890s. Even so, it came as a distinct surprise to see produced in Hitler's Germany no fewer than three Sherlock Holmes films, all in 1937. By that date the entire German film industry was under Nazi control. What subtle political messages from Dr Goebbels' propaganda machine could those films possibly have contained? The first was *Der Hund von Baskerville*, a seemingly straightforward adaptation of the old favourite, although brought up to date, with Sherlock Holmes in a polo-neck jersey and leather overcoat, prowling about a feudal-looking Schloss Baskerville. Maybe the message was about the decadence of the English aristocracy.

Certainly English highlife was the setting of the second film, released only one month later under the title *Sherlock Holmes: Die Graue Dame*. In this a bland chubby-faced character named Jimmy Ward, masquerading as a criminal, reveals himself as Sherlock Holmes, working with the Geheimpolizei; not by any remote chance based on a Conan Doyle story. The third and most remarkable film of this group, and one which has survived to be shown on West German television as recently as 1964, was *Der Mann, der Sherlock Holmes war* (The Man Who Was Sherlock Holmes). Throughout this extraordinary film the rather odd adventures of two characters purporting to be Sherlock Holmes and Dr Watson are constantly observed by a man who guffaws heartily every time they encounter him. Their adventures are so peculiar that eventually Holmes and Watson find themselves arrested and brought to trial. The mysterious man who laughs testifies that he is Conan Doyle and that Holmes and Watson never existed! The putative Sherlock Holmes in this strangely Pirandelloish story was Hans Albers, a popular German romantic film star of the 1930s and a certain box-office attraction.

The menacing shadow of war lay heavily across the continent, and no more Sherlock Holmes features would be made in Britain or Europe for twenty years.

Meanwhile, back at Twentieth Century-Fox . . .

CHAPTER 6

Basil Rathbone

Not that Basil Rathbone is not well suited to the role. He is, and would make, an ideal Holmes if the plays were put in period instead of being rather ludicrously brought up to date.

Lionel Collier, *Picturegoer* (1942)

If many of the published movie memoirs and reminiscences are to be believed, much of the casting in outstanding film roles has been casual and haphazard to say the least.

Apparently it was at a dinner party early in 1939 that Darryl F. Zanuck, then head of the Twentieth Century-Fox Studios, was in conversation with two of his colleagues. Basil Rathbone recalled the occasion:

> Gene Markey was one of his most distinguished writers and advisers, and Gregory Ratoff was an actor-director of prominence. Out of the blue Markey said, 'You know, someone ought to film Conan Doyle's classics, *The Adventures of Sherlock Holmes.*'
>
> Zanuck, I am told, immediately agreed but asked who should play Holmes, to which Markey replied, 'Basil Rathbone – who else?' Ratoff agreed enthusiastically but said they would need a Watson to complete the team. Thereupon Markey came up with my old friend Nigel Bruce. Then and there at the table the matter was settled and within a matter of days Nigel Bruce and I were both signed up to create these famous characters on film.

Not since Hal Roach teamed together Stan Laurel and Oliver Hardy has there been such an inspired piece of dual casting. Basil Rathbone, born in South Africa and raised in England, became a distinguished stage actor before going to America in the 1920s. He appeared in several silent films and when talking pictures were introduced, his incisive voice and distinct enunciation ensured for him a regular career in films. As often as not, he was cast as a villain and created some memorable bad characters in the thirties.

Nigel Bruce was another of the stage-trained British actors who had also gravitated to Hollywood, where they formed an English colony that seemed rather like a far-flung outpost of the empire. Their Englishness and their impeccable acting made them invaluable to the Hollywood system, since they could always be relied upon to improve any film in which they appeared. Bruce was habitually the dignified and slightly pompous English gentleman, and as Dr Watson he proved to be a marvellous foil to the Sherlock Holmes of Basil Rathbone.

Their first film, *The Hound of the Baskervilles*, was also their best, and arguably the best Sherlock Holmes film that has been made. With a generous budget, sensible casting and intelligent writing, *The Hound* remains an impressive mystery movie when seen more than thirty years later, and merits consideration at some length.

The screenplay stayed very close to Conan Doyle's original story, and for the first time on the screen a Sherlock Holmes adventure was set in the proper Victorian period. The period setting had an added significance in 1939, when a European war was imminent. Motion pictures are essentially escapist entertainment, and the nature of the escapism is conditioned by what one is trying to escape from. Hollywood had two noteworthy solutions at that time – lavish technicolour musicals and period-costume dramas, and *The Hound* fitted into the latter category very neatly.

The opulence of the sets and costumes was a little overdone for some tastes (Holmes's deerstalker and Inverness cape had obviously never been worn before), but this is a minor criticism of a splendid production. The eerie uneasy atmosphere of the fog-laden moors was impressively reproduced indoors on one of the Fox sound stages, and great care had been taken with all the sets to ensure authenticity. The script, by Ernest Pascal, was sympathetically written, and allowed the actors to develop their roles convincingly.

'Had I made but the one Holmes picture,' explained Basil Rathbone, 'I should probably not be as well known as I am today . . . Of all the adventures, *The Hound* is my favourite story, and it was in this picture that I had the stimulating experience of creating, within my own limited framework, a character that has intrigued me as much as any I have ever played.'

Basil Rathbone proved equal to the challenge of this intriguing character, and his performance as Sherlock Holmes was a revelation. He looked and behaved like the Sherlock Holmes that many of us visualise. In general, his portrayals of Holmes show a stronger, tenser, more sharply defined character than Arthur Wontner's, and yet both interpretations seem perfectly acceptable and convincing when seen in their separate contexts. Wontner was more the 'quiet thinker and logician of Baker Street', in Watson's words, with 'that tense far-away expression which I had learned to associate with the supreme manifestations of his genius'. Rathbone, on the other hand, with what Graham Greene described as 'that dark knife-blade face and snapping mouth', was the Holmes whose 'eager face still wore that expression of intense and high-strung energy'; whose keen incisive voice could lash like the crack of a whip at times of emergency; who, whenever the occasion demanded, was the most gentlemanly Sherlock Holmes of all. Rathbone consistently delivered his strong presentation of Holmes with such attack and vigour that he was always able to dominate the productions in which he appeared.

The story of *The Hound*, with its overtones of Gothic horror so popular with the Victorian reading public, is a fine exciting novel. Unlike the other three Sherlock Holmes long stories, the narrative is continuous, and is eminently suitable for adapting as a feature-length film. Finally, it follows the classic Sherlock Holmes story pattern of the leisurely introduction of Holmes and Watson in the Baker Street rooms, the arrival of an anxious client to relate a macabre tale, the preliminary investigation to pick up the scent, and the departure to the scene of yet another adventure.

On this occasion the clients are Dr Mortimer and the young Sir Henry Baskerville. Mortimer recounts the ancient legend of the ghostly hound, whose appearance always portends tragedy for the Baskerville family. Now that Sir Henry has inherited the title and property from his recently deceased uncle, strange things have been occurring, and Sherlock Holmes is asked to investigate. Pleading pressure of work,

Holmes sends Watson to accompany Dr Mortimer and Sir Henry to Dartmoor, while he remains in London. Watson, of course, is a decoy and Holmes is secretly in the vicinity all the time, much to the chagrin of Watson when he realises this. The villain of the piece is Stapleton, a near neighbour of Baskerville Hall, who turns out to be the long-lost cousin Roger Baskerville attempting to gain the inheritance by removing the other, more eligible, members of the family, using the family legend of the hound as a means to that end and as a cover for his activities. The grand climax of the story is the appearance of the hound itself, released by Stapleton to hunt down Sir Henry. Up to this point its existence has only been hinted at, referred to in local superstitions, and suspected from strange baying sounds heard from across the moor. The ghostly hound turns out to be a real hound, bedaubed with phosphorous, that has been kept hungry and savage out on the lonely mire, in which Stapleton eventually perishes.

The 1939 adaptation of this story for the screen made a number of alterations that were justified by the resultant production. Dr Mortimer in the film was older than in the book, and rather sinister in manner, but it was an improvement for the film to have more red herrings. (Mortimer was played by Lionel Atwill, who only the year before had portrayed the one-armed police chief opposite Rathbone's Dr Wolfgang Frankenstein in *The Son of Frankenstein*.) Another red herring was the presentation of Mrs Mortimer, who does not appear in the book, as a psychic medium.

Sir Henry Baskerville was played by Richard Greene, young, handsome, rising in popularity and obviously the right man on the studio payroll to provide the romantic lead and to get the girl (Stapleton's sister) in the final reel. Morton Lowry was an admirable Stapleton, really bringing to life 'that impassive colourless man . . . a creature of infinite patience and craft, with a smiling face and a murderous heart', as Doyle described him. An odd piece of casting was John Carradine as the butler Barrymore who in the film was renamed Barryman. It is said that this was done in deference to the acting family Barrymore.

The gaunt-faced Carradine was one of Fox's busiest character actors. Not long before *The Hound*, he was the man who shot Tyrone Power in the back in *Jesse James*; in John Ford's classic Western *Stagecoach* he was the Southern gambler Hatfield. Carradine was not too happy about the role of the butler: 'They made me wear a beard to make me look sinister. Of course no English butler ever wore a beard. But the idea was for the audience to say, "He did it! He did it!" as soon as they saw me. But I didn't; I was only the red herring. Movies sometimes use me just for that purpose.'

But it was Basil Rathbone and Nigel Bruce who really made the film the success it was. Assisted by good dialogue, their playing together established a believable relationship between the two characters. Fox were quick to spot this, and within eight months a second Sherlock Holmes film appeared, entitled *The Adventures of Sherlock Holmes*.

This second Holmes film by Fox was doubtless an economical project; hence the reappearance of some of the sets and five of the actors from the first film. Yet *The Adventures of Sherlock Holmes* bore no indications of hasty preparation. On the contrary, the whole film was as elaborately produced as *The Hound*, and was evidently planned in expectation of *The Hound*'s success. This time the scenario was not recognisably based on any Conan Doyle stories.

The Adventures began with an echo of the opening of Clive Brook's *Sherlock Holmes* (also made by Fox, in 1932), with Professor Moriarty in the dock at the Old Bailey. On this occasion, however, he is not convicted. 'According to the evidence we have heard,' says the foreman of the jury, 'we have no choice but to find the prisoner not guilty, and so find we all, and may God forgive us!' In similar vein, the judge comments on the verdict as 'a gross miscarriage of justice', and reluctantly discharges Moriarty. At that moment Sherlock Holmes bursts into the court with additional evidence, but to his disgust the professor has just been acquitted.

Holmes and Moriarty meet outside the court, and here the assured polished playing of Basil Rathbone and George Zucco is a sheer delight. 'May I give you a lift?' says Moriarty. 'Cabs are scarce in this rain.' As they ride along in the hansom they indulge in mutual vituperation in the most courteous manner possible, with Moriarty threatening to pull off a crime that will discredit Holmes.

The crime Moriarty is attempting is a project worthy of a master criminal – the theft of the Crown Jewels. Of course, the plot abounds in red herrings scattered by Moriarty, and Holmes pursues them all with great energy. In the customary episode depicting Sherlock Holmes the Master of Disguise, Holmes appears at a garden party as a hired music-hall entertainer, complete with false nose, straw boater and striped blazer, singing 'I Do Like to Be beside the Seaside'. (One can envisage somebody at Twentieth Century-Fox insisting on a musical number in the film, even if it had to be sung by Sherlock himself!) As a matter of disguise it is not very convincing, but as an impersonation of a music-hall turn it is a performance by Rathbone that is stunning in its accuracy of observation.

With all their faults, these two Fox films still provide enjoyable entertainment, largely because they were the stylish products of a big Hollywood studio when the studio system was at its peak. Fox's feature films had ample production values, and a professional finish to them that ensured a box-office profit. But it would have been untypical of Fox to tie themselves to a lengthy series, and they gave up their options.

However, Basil Rathbone and Nigel Bruce had been well and truly launched as the Holmes and Watson of the 1940s, for, following these two films they immediately began a highly successful series of weekly radio adventures that eventually ran for seven years in the USA.

After a while the film rights to the Sherlock Holmes stories were acquired by Universal Pictures, who placed under contract Rathbone, Bruce and Mary Gordon (the housekeeper, Mrs Hudson) as the principal members of the Baker Street *ménage*, in a partnership that lasted for four more years.

> Sherlock Holmes, the immortal character of fiction created by Sir Arthur Conan Doyle, is ageless and unchanging. In solving the significant problems of today he remains as ever the supreme master of deductive reasoning.

Thus ran the announcement at the beginning of the patriotic films which formed the second phase of Basil Rathbone's screen career as Sherlock Holmes. The choice of the word 'unchanging' in that context was most unfortunate. The film company had changed; Holmes had deteriorated into a rather fussy neurotic type of character; a fatuous bumbling Watson was largely relegated to providing comic relief, and the films had sunk to the category of B pictures.

In a period of patriotic near-hysteria, the desire to show fiction's best-known character performing his war service is quite understand-able. Conan Doyle himself had done the same thing with Sherlock Holmes during the Great War, in the short story *His Last Bow*. But surely only the Hollywood that produced the blonde-in-the-bomber type of epic rubbish could have conceived the three films that ensued.

The first of these, *Sherlock Holmes and The Voice of Terror*, was perhaps the most unhappy choice of subjects of all Holmes films. It concerned the running to earth of an English traitor broadcasting sub-versive propaganda from a secret radio station, and assisting in a projected invasion of England. In 1942 the people of Great Britain were very touchy about treachery, anti-British broadcasts and invasion, and there was obviously concern about exhibiting the film, which was not released until nearly a year after the second film, *Sherlock Holmes and the Secret Weapon*. In this, Holmes is engaged to guard the Swiss inventor of a new bomb-sight which the Nazis are after. They recruit to their service none other than Professor Moriarty, this time played by Lionel Atwill, lately Dr Mortimer. Apart from the Holmes–Moriarty conflict, there is nothing in the film that distinguishes it from all the other topical crime-and-spy films of the early war years.

In fact the one aspect of the Universal series upon which everyone agrees is that they were undistinguished. Having brought Sherlock Holmes up to date to take part in the Second World War, they could not revert to an earlier period when the war ended. Nor, one suspects, would they have spent the necessary money to do so. So the series remained firmly in the B-picture category.

At the end of *Secret Weapon*, Holmes and Watson, having saved the bomb-sight, watch numbers of bombers flying by as Holmes quotes Shakespeare's 'This blessed plot . . .'

In *Sherlock Holmes in Washington*, a Holmes who smoked only cigar-ettes took a little accepting, as did the extraordinary drooping locks of hair on the temples.

The story concerned one of those vital documents which are always liable to cause the downfall of at least an empire if they find their way into the wrong hands, and yet which never seem to be accorded any more security than a bus ticket, to judge from the frequency with which they go astray.

This particular document is on microfilm, and is carried as far as

Washington before its bearer is murdered by members of a spy ring. He has, of course, already planted the microfilm elsewhere, and the remainder of the film is taken up by the race between Sherlock Holmes and the spy ring to obtain it. At the close of the film Holmes and Watson drive past back-projected views of Washington while Holmes quotes from Mr Winston Churchill's speech to Congress in December 1941: 'It is not given to us to peer into the mysteries of the future. Still . . . in the days to come the British and American peoples will for their own safety and for the good of all walk together side by side in majesty, in justice and in peace.' This sentiment appears to have been the sole motive for making *Sherlock Holmes in Washington* at all.

Fortunately the Second World War ended before we could be subjected to any more sorry examples of Sherlock Holmes's celluloid war service. In 1944, with the end of the war in sight, Universal presented *Sherlock Holmes Faces Death*, a title reminiscent of the early years of the movies. The screenplay was based on the short story *The Musgrave Ritual*, and at times the similarity between Basil Rathbone in certain poses and some of the later Sidney Paget illustrations was quite surprising. An extremely effective addition to the Ritual was the introduction of an allusive chess problem, which Holmes solved on the huge black and white stone-slabbed floor of the Hall. This sequence lent itself to some dramatic grouping in the composition of the scene.

Inspector Lestrade, played by Dennis Hoey, appeared in this film. He had already been in *Sherlock Holmes and the Secret Weapon*, and he appeared in another four films. Hoey's Lestrade was a policeman of almost unbelievable stupidity. That is not meant to disparage Mr Hoey's acting. In all six films he played the part of a stupid policeman very well, but it is just impossible to believe in such a character as the script writers depicted. He was arrogant, ignorant, badly spoken, insufferably rude to everyone, and at times cautioned people that 'anything they say will be used against them'. Detective story writers learned to avoid that one years ago. Such characterisation only weakened the effect of these films. Nothing was added to Holmes's stature by his solution of problems which an idiot of a policeman bungled.

The next film in the Basil Rathbone series was *Spider Woman*, allegedly 'based on a story by Sir Arthur Conan Doyle'. It dealt with a mysterious succession of suicides brought about by a woman who secures insurance on her victims' lives and then introduces into their bedrooms a huge spider, the venom from which produces such agony that the victims are forced to self-destruction. Gale Sondergaard, a familiar female villain in films of the forties, played the title role. As is often the case with the better villains, *Spider Woman* was resurrected for a film sequel, not involving Holmes.

The Scarlet Claw which followed, was a surrender to the style of sensational crime magazines. One cinema trade journal described it as 'proceeding on established Hollywood lines of ably suggested horror', and indeed the settings looked very similar to those of *The Wolf Man*, made by Universal around that time.

The action took place in a village in Canada, where killings by a legendary monster turned out to be the work of a maniac with a steel claw. 'Ably suggested horror' is an apt way of describing the work of the producer-director of the series, Roy William Neill, for a number of the screenplays were plainly sensational and moderately horrific. Like the actors he directed, Neill had to contend with some frightful material, and it is to his credit that he was able to create atmosphere and drama out of absurdities. Although all the films in this series were B pictures, it is due to Neill's long experience and visual technique that the films were much better than could reasonably have been expected.

Three of the Universal films had limited settings; the crimes and the suspects were confined to a particular place, and the investigations largely a process of elimination. Thus the films were economical to make, with a small number of sets for interior scenes and a liberal use of stock shots from the studio library for the exteriors.

The House of Fear, set in a standard lonely house atmosphere, was said to be based on the story *The Five Orange Pips*. The only connection was the use of orange pips as death warnings to the group of men living in the house who are murdered one after another. The solution, which Holmes stumbles across, to the explosive annoyance of Lestrade, is that the men are all alive and waiting to collect a great deal of insurance money.

In *Pursuit to Algiers*, Holmes was employed to escort a young monarch on his way to being restored to his Ruritanian throne. Almost the whole of the action takes place on board ship, and the appearance of Morton Lowry as a ship's steward immediately gives the game away. The king Holmes is escorting is, of course, a decoy and the steward is the real king. Slightly better in content, but almost as improbable, was *Terror by Night*, in which Holmes is engaged to escort a famous diamond on its train journey from Euston to Edinburgh. Also on the train are the tiresome Lestrade and Colonel Moran, played by Alan Mowbray (who was Inspector Lestrade himself years before, in *A Study in Scarlet*). The diamond is stolen soon after the journey begins, and the usual murders and recovery ensue. An interesting point was the way in which fair play in the displaying of clues was observed on at least one occasion. Holmes asks to see the diamond at the beginning of the journey, and later, when the theft has occurred, he produces the diamond from his breast pocket and announces that the stolen jewel is an imitation, substituted by him when he was examining the original. If one cared to sit the film round again, this was found to be quite true, and quite a neat sleight-of-hand job Rathbone made of it.

A brighter interlude was *The Pearl of Death* which was an adaptation of *The Six Napoleons*, the short story in which the hunt takes place for the famous Black Pearl of the Borgias, hidden in one of six plaster busts of Napoleon. The film was filled out by being prefaced with some adventures of the pearl before its insertion in the bust.

The Pearl of Death and *Sherlock Holmes Faces Death* were the only modernised films in the Basil Rathbone series to make serious attempts to follow existing stories by Conan Doyle. The remainder occasionally borrowed incidents and ideas from the stories. Several carried the admission that they were only 'based on the characters created by Sir Arthur Conan Doyle'.

Hypnosis, blackmail and a series of diabolical murders, comparable with those of Jack the Ripper, were some of the rich ingredients of *The Woman in Green*. The interview scene between Holmes and Moriarty in Baker Street was reproduced in this film in word and spirit, and Henry Daniell matched very well Doyle's description of Moriarty's 'soft, precise fashion of speech' which left 'a conviction of sincerity which a mere bully could not produce'. It was a pity that Basil Rathbone's Holmes was not pitted against Henry Daniell's Moriarty in a more worthy screenplay.

Basil Rathbone made his last bow on the screen in *Dressed to Kill*, which concerned the manufacture, by a convict in Dartmoor, of musical boxes which contain in their tunes a coded message to confederates outside, telling them the whereabouts of a set of plates for printing £5 notes. The hiding-place turns out to be in the Dr Johnson Memorial House in Gough Square. The film was an improvement in a series that had declined sadly.

This third group of Basil Rathbone's portrayals consisted of nine films, all made between 1944 and 1946. The wonderfully detailed Baker Street room must have been a permanent fixture on the Universal set, and so must many of the supporting actors who appeared quite a few times in these films. Some of them appeared so often that the series began to seem like an involved serial. Indeed, in Germany four of the films were cannibalised to produce two large feature films, an operation that must have had extraordinary results. The modernisation of Holmes's appearance was reasonably good; Watson seemed to have aged quite a lot by comparison. The English settings seemed to hover uncertainly around the 1920s, as did the men's clothes. The women's clothes, on the other hand, were always currently fashionable.

The Baker Street set made a fleeting guest appearance in the 1943 film *Crazy House*. Universal had already made a film version of Olsen and Johnson's *Hellzapoppin*, a zany show that made the Marx Brothers look like a Sunday School lesson. *Crazy House* began at the Universal Studios with news being received of Olsen and Johnson returning. There is immediate panic; staff run in all directions, and the film swiftly switches from set to set. Andy Devine gallops through a Western town crying 'Olsen and Johnson are coming!'; in another Western scene Leo Carrillo warns his amigos that Olsen and Johnson are coming; Dr Watson bursts into the Baker Street room, and Sherlock Holmes says, 'I know, Watson. Olsen and Johnson are coming.'

'How do you know?'

'I am Sherlock Holmes. I know everything.'

Throughout the Universal series Basil Rathbone and Nigel Bruce continued their weekly adventures on the NBC Blue radio network. Some of the stories were from Conan Doyle, but many were specially contrived by a number of skilled radio dramatists, and outstanding among these was Edith Meiser, *the* pioneer. She first thought of a

Page 87 (above) Kenneth Macmillan and company in the ballet *The Great Detective* (1953); (below) on the set at Shepperton Studios: Dr Watson (Donald Houston), Sherlock Holmes (John Neville) and director James Hill, right front.
A Study in Terror (Compton-Cameo, 1965)

$$E = mc^2$$

$$(a+b)^n = a^n + na^{n-1}b \ldots$$

$$\frac{n(n-1)(n-2)}{3!}$$

Page 88 (above) Sherlock
Holmes (Fritz Weaver) and
Irene Adler (Inga Swenson) are
held captive by Professor
Moriarty (Martin Gabel) in the
New York musical *Baker Street*
(1965). The blackboard joke
implies the brilliant Moriarty's
anticipation of Einstein's theory
(*left*) Robert Stephens
and Colin Blakely in *The
Private Life of Sherlock Holmes*
(Mirisch, 1970)

Sherlock Holmes radio series in 1927, and had to write to England for a complete set of the stories, since they were not all in print in the USA. It took Miss Meiser more than a year to find a sponsor willing to back her idea. She wrote the first radio programme in 1930, and continued writing for the various series until the middle 1940s. Her adaptations and original plays were very faithful to the spirit of the Baker Street traditions, and also well constructed radio plays. Many of them were produced by her husband, Tom McKnight.

The popularity of the Conan Doyle stories in the USA was enhanced by the various successful American radio series, which also influenced the movie makers, who were fond of cashing in on radio favourites in the 1930s. The attitude of the Conan Doyle Estate was extremely liberal towards American presentations on radio, and later on television, and adapters enjoyed a greater freedom there than elsewhere. Thus Edith Meiser and her fellow writers were able to use scores of plots and stories of their own, once the original tales had been exhausted, but they observed the simple ground rule of non-modernisation. It was customary for Dr Watson to narrate the stories to the programme announcer, but he was always reminiscing about events of the Victorian age, recaptured for the radio audience by plentiful sound effects of horsedrawn vehicles and other noises.

On one occasion Basil Rathbone and Nigel Bruce appeared as guests on a comedy radio show and swapped their regular parts, with Rathbone as a bumbling Watson and Bruce as a sharp decisive Holmes. It is reported that Rathbone's imitation of Nigel Bruce stopped the show. But then Rathbone was such a talented actor that he could deal with that sort of situation with ease; such a talented actor that he felt Sherlock Holmes had blighted his career:

> I was deeply concerned with the problem of being 'typed', more completely 'typed' than any other classic actor has ever been or ever will be again. My fifty-two roles in twenty-three plays of Shakespeare, my years in the London and New York theater, my scores of motion pictures, including my two Academy Award nominations, were slowly but surely sinking into oblivion: and there was nothing I could do about it, except to stop playing Mr. Holmes, which I could not do owing to the existence of a long term contract.

When his contracts came up for renewal he refused to continue in the role in films or on radio. But it was too late. He never really had another starring role, and his career did sink into oblivion. So after seven years he tried a comeback, appearing once more as Sherlock Holmes in a single programme in the CBS Television *Suspense* series in 1953. Later that same year he appeared on the stage in *Sherlock Holmes*, a play written for him by his wife Ouida; but her play turned out to be an even more abject failure than *The Holmeses of Baker Street*, for it ran on Broadway for only three days!

The only other impersonator to move from screen to stage, Eille Norwood, had crowned his long series of films with a triumphant stage production, but Basil Rathbone's last Sherlock Holmes film had been seven years before the play, and it had been left too late.

The loss on the production must have been enormous, for the play was spectacularly mounted, with Professor Moriarty falling into the Reichenbach Falls from the balcony of a Swiss villa. The reviews were fairly unanimous that the play was cumbersome and not well constructed; it had too many characters, and the acting left much to be desired. 'On the whole,' wrote one critic, '*Sherlock Holmes* is an occasion for regret. It would have been wonderful to have the master back with us.' Another reviewer pointed out one of the main reasons for failure: 'It is a loose plot for a public geared to the stopwatch timing of a TV thriller.' Television was already an immense influence in the USA by 1953, and the play really *was* too late.

Towards the end of his life, Basil Rathbone made a number of gramophone records of readings from various classics, and naturally some of these were Sherlock Holmes stories. He was thus the only actor to span all five of the entertainment media – stage, screen, radio, television and records – covered by this catalogue. The readings are a little variable in quality, and the voice has lost some of its former crispness; nevertheless the recordings form a pleasant and unusual souvenir of this outstanding actor. But for vintage Rathbone there is one LP that has everything: it is an NBC broadcast of 1939, when the actors were still fresh in their roles; it is a Conan Doyle story; it is adapted by Edith Meiser; for good measure it has Nigel Bruce stumbling over his lines. It is difficult to imagine any finer helping of dramatised Holmesian nostalgia.

CHAPTER 7

His Latest Bows

The impression that Holmes was a real person of flesh and blood may have been intensified by his frequent appearances upon the stage.

Conan Doyle

The 1930s and 1940s were a Golden Age of Radio in the USA and the various series of weekly half-hour broadcast adventures of Sherlock Holmes were an important part of that great era. Not so in Britain, where the BBC thought so little of the Holmes stories that there was no regular series until 1952, and then only monthly in *Children's Hour*. There had been occasional broadcasts from about the 1940s, with such notable performers as Arthur Wontner and Sir Cedric Hardwicke in the role of Sherlock Holmes. The 1952 series progressed to a short-run weekly evening series, followed by many others, in which practically all the stories by Conan Doyle were given. In these series Carleton Hobbs and Norman Shelley became established as BBC Radio's Holmes and Watson. They performed in an adaptation of William Gillette's *Sherlock Holmes* in 1953. Scenes from this play were also given in the first stereophonic radio drama to be broadcast, in 1958.

In 1954 Harry Alan Towers devised and produced a series of twelve Sherlock Holmes radio plays as a commercial venture, and sold them to the BBC and American and overseas networks. The series was clearly cast to sell on the names of the principal actors, for it had Sir John Gielgud as Sherlock Holmes and Sir Ralph Richardson as Dr Watson, and all the plays were adaptations of Conan Doyle stories. The beautifully modulated Gielgud voice was matched with the homelier ruminating tones of Ralph Richardson, and the series was written with considerable imagination. In the last programme of the series the two distinguished principals were joined by Orson Welles as Professor Moriarty, sounding like an oily Victorian Harry Lime.

(Orson Welles was a highly experienced actor on radio, and in 1938 his Mercury Theatre on the Air Company was giving weekly Sunday evening broadcast versions of great classics. One of these, *The War of the Worlds*, became notorious for the sensation and panic it caused, and just one month before that the Mercury company performed Gillette's *Sherlock Holmes* with Orson Welles in the title role.)

It was unusual for the BBC to use programmes made elsewhere, but by 1954 steam radio, as it began to be called, was rapidly losing talent to television, the cuckoo in the nest, and was glad to buy out programmes when it could. The swift spread of television was threatening the cinema as well and there was no longer any such creature as the regular filmgoer, habitually visiting his local cinema once or twice a week. Realisation of this came rather slowly and agonisingly to the film industry, which eventually evolved a sort of twofold compromise with its deadly rival. Firstly, thousands of old films from the vaults were, and still are, sold to television companies as ready-made entertainment. Secondly, studio space was reallocated to making films specifically for television, and television audiences soon developed an appetite for various long-running series featuring familiar characters week after week; not quite soap-operas, but succeeding on the same premise.

So in thirty years the cycle in Sherlock Holmes films came right round again to a long series of short films, this time made specifically for television in 1953 and 1954, by an American company, Guild Films, with Ronald Howard and Howard Marion Crawford as Holmes and Watson.

Ronald Howard inherited the good looks of his famous father Leslie Howard and, like his father, he has suffered at times from having too youthful an appearance for many of the roles he has had to play. He was certainly a rather lightweight Holmes, especially against Howard Marion Crawford's rather hefty Watson. The series of thirty-nine films was made in France, with casts of English and French actors, although the principals did come to England to film a number of exterior scenes with authentic London backgrounds.

The pilot of the series, *The Case of the Cunningham Heritage*, contained the only version on film of the first meeting between Holmes and Watson at St Bartholomew's Hospital. The occasion was relieved of pomposity by Watson's discovery, after they have shaken hands, that they have been doing so right in the path of a jet of steam from one of Holmes's chemical experiments. They move into the Baker Street rooms and get to know one another, very much in the spirit of the opening chapter of *A Study in Scarlet*, and very neatly setting the stage for the future episodes. Unfortunately, the series did not live up to its promising start. Only a few films were based on Conan Doyle stories, of which perhaps the closest adaptation was *The Red-Headed League*. Filming was evidently carried out on a low budget, and the quality of the writing was very variable. Character actor Harry Towb recalled appearing in a couple of films in the series:

A lot of them were written by Americans. At that time there were a lot of expatriate Hollywood writers living there who had suffered from the un-American activities committee, and that was one of the ways they made a living . . . They shot each of the films in four days. They used to pay in francs – 50,000 francs for the four days, which was £50. They paid your fare, but you had to pay your own expenses, so you didn't make much from it . . . but I must say they were super to work for. They shot them very quickly. It wasn't really quality stuff. Shelley Reynolds was a clever director though, because to shoot 27 minutes or so in four days was some going. They were great fun, but they were really an excuse to go to Paris!

The Baker Street set, built inside one of the Poste Parisien Studios, was narrow and quaint, with an un-English lamp-post outside 221B that seems to have been moved up and down the street to suit the cameraman. In one episode it had been moved along to give a better view of a Western covered waggon that was parked there. That was in *The Texas Cowgirl*, which also included such oddities as a tepee erected *inside* the Baker Street rooms and a Red Indian chief in full dress, all apparently from a travelling Wild West show.

Other banalities can be imagined from titles like *The Baker Street Nursemaids* and *The Baker Street Bachelors*. The poor material was a great handicap to a lively producing and acting team, and regrettably the series could hardly be rated very highly. It was never shown on

British television, which had already tried a short series of six plays, three years earlier.

This series of six adaptations of Conan Doyle stories was televised by the BBC in 1951, and at that time the plays were transmitted live, so that on occasions it was necessary to endure the intermittent sounds of scene shifters that accompanied some of the quieter and more tense moments. Alan Wheatley gave a scholarly and enjoyable performance as Sherlock Holmes, aided by a first-class Dr Watson, played by Raymond Francis, who later became famous as Detective Chief Superintendent Lockhart of the television series *No Hiding Place*. In his book *Writing for Television Today*, Arthur Swinson comments on this particular series of plays, and on the unsuitability of the original dialogue of the stories, which is very much a written dialogue, rather than a spoken dialogue. The adaptations were by C. A. Lejeune, film critic of *The Observer*, and Swinson remarks that even after half a lifetime telling others how to write and act, an experienced person like Miss Lejeune could fall into the trap. Alan Wheatley certainly bears this out:

> I must say I found it the most difficult thing to speak that I've ever done in the whole of my career . . . She also did some things that again really she shouldn't have fallen into – technical things like not allowing anything like enough time for changes. Of course, television was all live in those days, and in one particular scene, which I'll never forget, she finished up one scene with a sentence from me, and opened the next scene with a sentence from me, *in a heavy disguise*, with no time at all, and they could not think of a way of altering this. The only thing we could do was for me to play the previous scene out of camera while I was making-up in the corner of the set, and that was a nightmare, playing the lines from one scene and trying to change my make-up out of shot. But it created quite a lot of comment, because people thought – how on earth was that done? At the time it certainly was a successful series, and it had an enormous amount of publicity.

Curiously, the BBC never followed up this series, and when they finally got round to Sherlock Holmes again, fourteen years later, they acted as if they had never heard of Ian Atkins's productions.

Earlier, in 1951, a projected series of films for television had been commenced in England, but only the first film was ever made. It was an adaptation of the short story *The Man with the Twisted Lip* and again was set in the Victorian period. The film slipped into supporting programmes on general release, and was never heard of again.

As a counter-attraction to television, the film industry has resorted to larger and more spectacular films in a variety of forms, whilst still turning out a much reduced number of conventional feature films. As already observed, the Sherlock Holmes story most suited to a feature-length film is *The Hound of the Baskervilles*, its only disadvantage being that it is also the most filmed Holmes story. The version presented by Hammer Films in 1959 was the seventh, and the makers clearly felt obliged to do something different with it. In the space of three or four years Hammer had earned themselves an international reputation for turning out a string of horror films of the Frankenstein and Dracula type that were financially very successful and cinematically rather distasteful. So it was fully expected that their production of *The Hound of the Baskervilles* would be an attempt at a blood-curdler. The story is certainly strong enough to withstand such treatment. However, there must have been a bad attack of cold feet, for when the film finally emerged it was neither a full-blooded horror film nor a straight dramatised version of the original novel ('Doyle and water,' commented one critic). The story and characters had been tampered with extensively and unnecessarily, and the natural dramatic (and horrific) climax of the plot – the appearance of the Hound itself – showed us a dog that would have been hard put to scare a small child.

Peter Cushing was presented as a very dandified Holmes, and when he did appear in the regulation costume of deerstalker and cape he looked to be wearing garments several sizes too large; the role of Sherlock Holmes seemed to be too large as well and although Mr Cushing's performance had been very carefully studied he was not helped by very poor, humourless material. That, together with his rather cool style of acting, did not result in a convincing portrayal. André Morrell was a very good, restrained Dr Watson. The film is notable for being the first Sherlock Holmes screen adventure in colour.

With a broadside of publicity customarily reserved for soap-opera favourites and pop-star productions, the BBC launched a series of twelve Sherlock Holmes television plays in 1965, which were repeated in 1966.

In recent years BBC Television have shown themselves to be masters in recapturing the atmosphere of many periods in English history, and this series proved to be no exception. The late-Victorian environment was recreated with loving care – such loving care in fact that the producers could not tear themselves away from it, and the lingering looks at all the settings and locations slowed down the pace of most of the episodes, all of which were adapted from Doyle stories to a fifty-minute programme length, when thirty to forty minutes would have sufficed.

The plays were extremely well done by a team of professional television writers, and the casting of practically all the supporting players was admirable. The choice of Douglas Wilmer as Sherlock Holmes was widely argued, but was generally felt to have been a little disappointing, particularly after the big build-up. Wilmer's Holmes did not come across as a sufficiently sympathetic character, although meticulously carried out. Nigel Stock's Dr Watson was well done, and he managed to avoid slipping into a faithful-puppy-dog treatment of the part.

In 1968 a further television series was presented by the BBC. Douglas Wilmer was replaced by Peter Cushing, while Nigel Stock remained as Watson. For years Peter Cushing has pursued a career in the Hammer horror films, and it seems that the BBC brought him in to play Holmes on the strength of that experience. The aspects of horror and violence that obtruded throughout the series were not only deliberately calculated by the producers, but were proudly heralded in the BBC's advance publicity, some of which read as follows:

> What is new in this series is the basic approach – a daring realisation of the lurking horror and callous savagery of Victorian crime, especially sexual crime. Here is the re-creation of the Victorian half-world of brutal males and the furtive innocents they dominate; of evil-hearted servants scheming and embracing below stairs; of murder, mayhem and the macabre as the hansom cab once again sets out with Dr. Watson and his debonair, eccentric and uncannily observant friend – Mr. Sherlock Holmes.

In general this series was bad enough to make one feel guilty of a lack of gratitude for the carefully made Wilmer series of 1965. The adaptations were slanted to emphasise the 'lurking horror and callous savagery' described above, and at times the productions appeared amateurish in the extreme. Peter Cushing's Holmes was amazingly variable and clearly suffered from the extremely compressed production schedules and generally disappointing direction. But Nigel Stock developed his portrayal of Dr Watson very attractively and was a considerable help in saving the series from total failure. It was sad to see that the standards of the BBC had deteriorated so much in just three years.

In the field of Sherlock Holmes studies, there has been advanced an intriguing notion that must have exercised the minds of many Holmesians – that Sherlock Holmes and his great adversary Professor Moriarty were one and the same person: a sort of Jekyll and Hyde manifestation, showing alternately a brilliant criminologist and a brilliant criminal in conflict with each other.

In 1953 Margaret Dale and Richard Arnell took the idea a step further by boldly presenting it in the form of a ballet. It was called *The Great Detective* and was staged at Sadlers Wells with Kenneth Macmillan in the role of Holmes and Moriarty.

The subtitle described the piece as 'A Ballet after Sir A. Conan Doyle, introducing typical characters and featuring the struggle for supremacy between the Great Detective and his Arch Enemy, the Infamous Professor.' On the stage, having one performer in both roles made the customary confrontation between the two protagonists somewhat difficult to effect, and thus the ballet was not able to convey the 'struggle for supremacy' very satisfactorily. The Press made much of the novelty of a Sherlock Holmes ballet, but it was not taken very seriously.

They Might Be Giants was not so much a Sherlock Holmes adventure as a related piece, intended to illuminate some of life's problems by using the Sherlock Holmes convention. It did not succeed as a play, nor later as a film, because of a lack of dramatic construction to carry through the play's theme to any sort of conclusion. This was unfortunate, because the plot contained some interesting situations, and passages of highly amusing satire, dealing as it did with an American judge, Justin Playfair, who imagines he is Sherlock Holmes, roaming New York City on a supposedly moral and philosophical journey of detection. His brother, who is being blackmailed, wants him certified in order to get at his money. The lady psychiatrist engaged to do the certifying is a Dr Mildred Watson, no less, and after attempting, and failing, to analyse and treat Playfair, she ends up joining his crusade, and the piece ends with them in a cascade of light, looking as if, like the play, they were overwhelmed by the symbolism and the whimsy of it all.

The play was intended as a New York production, but this pre-Broadway try-out at Joan Littlewood's Theatre Workshop was one of her few experiments at that time that failed. 'Even Miss Littlewood,' said one reviewer, 'can make a mistake.'

The same American producer, Harold Prince, who had planned *They Might Be Giants* for New York, looked to have made another mistake when he directed a new musical based on the adventures of Sherlock Holmes. On the face of it *Baker Street* sounded like the musical least likely to succeed, but the musical has now broken free from the corsets of 'nice' musical comedy set in Ruritania, and has become a vehicle for social comment and for presenting clashes of personalities in hitherto unexpected settings, often with an historical basis.

Jerome Coopersmith compiled a story which included all the essential ingredients for a popular Sherlock Holmes stage drama – a bold crime, an arch-criminal (Professor Moriarty again), some love interest (Irene Adler again) some dramatic action and some spectacular settings. Of course, all these elements had been present in Ouida Rathbone's play, too, but Mr Coopersmith deliberately disregarded the traditional solemnity of the subject and, aided by the music of Raymond Jessel and Marian Grudeff, turned out a show that sounds to have been big, brassy and boisterous.

At the time of writing, we have not yet had the opportunity of seeing *Baker Street* in Great Britain, and therefore we can only judge from an imported long-playing record and a copy of Mr Coopersmith's libretto. *The New York Daily News* described it as 'An absolutely captivating entertainment.' The American show-business periodical *Variety* said: 'Splendid is the word for *Baker Street*, a big rousing success in the *My Fair Lady*, *Around the World in 80 Days* class.' This reference to *My Fair Lady* is interesting, because the resemblance seems very strong. The style of the music and songs (and even the LP cover) is similar, and both musicals have a celibate hero who semi-speaks his songs and who eventually succumbs to the charms of the heroine. The similarities between *Baker Street* and *My Fair Lady* can be traced back a long way. In his play *Pygmalion*, first produced in 1913, Bernard

Shaw followed quite closely the Holmes and Watson pattern of relationship for Professor Higgins and Colonel Pickering. Pickering, a very proper, respectable ex-military gentleman, is the perfect foil for Higgins, and is frequently trying to keep the genius's feet on the ground and to soften his impact on the world at large – very much the Watson role. Higgins, although far ruder in his behaviour than Holmes, is a highly trained observer of dialects and phonetics, and can place any man by his voice within six miles – within two miles in London. He is even the author of a book on the subject. With his fund of specialised knowledge and his preoccupied behaviour, he is, in his way, almost too Holmesian to be true. So it is really hardly surprising that a Sherlock Holmes musical should resemble *My Fair Lady*, which in any case influenced much that came after it.

To succeed with the somewhat preposterous story of *Baker Street*, Jerome Coopersmith indulges in an irreverent tongue-in-cheek approach to the established conventions of the Holmesian canon, and it seems to work. Like most American musicals it has a verve and drive that carry one over the shortcomings of the piece, although it abounds in specimens of Broadway Cockney that startle the English ear. As a light-hearted entertainment it sounds most enjoyable. As an experiment in a new Sherlockian stage-form, it certainly seems to have been worth doing.

The preliminary announcements stated that Holmes would be played by Fritz Weaver and Dr Watson by Peter Sallis, misreported by some newspapers as Peter Sellers. 'It happens all the time with me,' said Peter Sallis, resignedly, when he discussed the musical:

> I think it's extremely difficult to assess why a thing is a success or why it is a failure. I don't think that *Baker Street* was a failure, but it was a failure financially, which is unfortunately the criterion. It ran on Broadway for something like nine months, which, as we now know, is not enough. Alex Cohen (the producer) is a terrific showman. The Broadway Theatre was done up like a dog's dinner. He had life-size working cut-outs of the characters above the awning outside the theatre, in an enormous scene, all worked by electricity. It was in constant action all the time the show was on . . . I cannot *tell* you the amount of money that was poured into it. The sets were brilliant, and we had this puppet thing – they dropped a cloth down and across the cloth was a painted scene of London with all the obvious landmarks, and you saw this little carriage drawn by eight horses

with Queen Victoria in it, bowing; this was all done by marionettes – I remember it because I used to have to sit behind it every night and the cloth would go up and there were Fritz and I, we were the next scene – and the roar of applause from the audience when they began to realise what was happening! It must have cost a fortune. It was a brilliant idea, and because they were puppets it had a sort of magic about it. All the settings were marvellous. Now, you can flash moments of brilliance like that at an audience, but it's the show as a whole that is either going to carry it or not . . . Possibly the mistake they made was in concentrating so much on Irene Adler at the expense of Moriarty. Irene Adler is a red herring in the sense that Holmes doesn't even get the girl in the end. If the book of *Baker Street* did have a flaw then perhaps it was that, because, if you know anything abut Holmes at all, you're expecting Holmes and Moriarty, and, let's face it, in *Baker Street* we dodged about a great deal for about an hour or more before Moriarty appeared, and Irene was there from the beginning of the show right through to the end. It was more a will-he won't-he play about Holmes and Adler than it was about Holmes and Moriarty . . . But then of course you get down to the problem that it *is* a musical and you can't have two chaps singing at each other, one as the hero and the other as the villain, ad nauseam for the whole of the evening. So perhaps the answer is that you can't make a musical of Sherlock Holmes.

Two principals from the Hammer *Hound* were concerned with the next Holmes film to appear, which was *Sherlock Holmes und das Halsband des Todes* (Sherlock Holmes and the Necklace of Death), made in Berlin in 1962; the Hammer personnel involved were the director Terence Fisher and the actor Christopher Lee, who had been Sir Henry Baskerville in the *Hound* and was now Sherlock Holmes, together with another English actor, Thorley Walters, as Dr Watson. All the rest of the cast, the production team and the style of the film were German.

The film was set in London in a period that wavered between Edwardian and 1930s. The story, by Curt Siodmak, was partly based on *The Valley of Fear* and Professor Moriarty appears and takes part in the skulduggery, although the very idea of his implication is scorned by Herr Inspektor Cooper, who is, of course, completely baffled. In a curious finish to the film, Sherlock Holmes finally retrieves the necklace, but completely fails to incriminate Moriarty, leaving him available for a possible sequel.

The tall impressive figure of Christopher Lee, a frequent Hammer

Count Dracula, looked quite well as Sherlock Holmes; Thorley Walters rather reminded one of an Edwardian Avenger – a sort of John Steed with moustache. Terence Fisher's plodding direction, so evident in the Hammer *The Hound*, was continued, uninspired and humourless in the second film. There had been such a long period after the Rathbone series with no feature films at all, that the lack of entertainment in these two films proved doubly disappointing. It was a low watermark in Holmes sound films.

When the recovery came, it was magnificent. Sir Nigel Films, a company formed by the Sir Arthur Conan Doyle Estate to film his works, produced *A Study in Terror*, a story of the successful solution of the Jack-the-Ripper murders by Sherlock Holmes, and it was one of the best-made Holmes films there has been. It had practically everything in its favour, with a first-class screenplay by Donald and Derek Ford; smooth assured direction by James Hill; and excellent casting and acting. The beautiful photography in subdued colour was keyed to the atmosphere of the sordid Whitechapel environment, and the poignancy was heightened by a simple theme tune in the background music, trite but haunting, which emphasised the essential sadness of the ghastly tale.

The horribly brutal murders were treated very realistically without being offensive – no mean achievement in a plot that included the circumstances of the real murders that terrorised Whitechapel in 1888. The superb writing of the Fords was done with good taste, style, careful attention to the Holmesian conventions, and some well-placed humour to lighten the sombre subject. One source of humour was Sherlock's brother Mycroft Holmes, played by Robert Morley, who anticipates the prime minister's request for help when the gruesome crimes become a political issue:

'Mycroft, I've sent for you because you have the tidiest and most orderly brain in Her Majesty's Civil Service.'

'Prime Minister, I cannot deny it!'

Inspector Lestrade, on the wrong track as ever, is also a source of humour, but he is not treated as an idiot, and as played by Frank Finlay is entirely believable. He emerges from the room of one of the victims, to be met by Holmes, who asks: 'Lestrade, my dear fellow; are you not well?' Lestrade, clearly shaken up, wearily replies, 'You'll never see anything like it, this side of hell. What animal could have done this?' We, too, feel shaken at that moment in the film, and the whole subtle treatment of the Whitechapel atrocities is an object lesson to all modern horror film makers who seem to want their achievements measured in buckets of gore.

Donald Houston as Dr Watson, was brave, loyal and willing, but baffled, lacking imagination and woefully out of his depth. The intelligent writing and direction of his role enabled Houston to present a really enjoyable foil to Holmes, rather than a fool. The whole relationship between Holmes and Watson, as revealed in their conversations and actions, was highly satisfactory. For the first time since Rathbone and Bruce one could believe that these men shared their lodgings and knew each other well.

And Sherlock Holmes? All the best Sherlock Holmeses have been experienced stage actors, irrespective of the medium in which they performed as Holmes, and John Neville was certainly no exception. He was already a leading Shakespearian player before he became the director of the Nottingham Playhouse, from where he travelled daily by aeroplane to Shepperton while much of the filming was going on. His performance as Sherlock Holmes was extremely good; a crisp and lively impersonation. And yet it did just lack that electric spark between actor and audience.

With the cost of feature film production rising all the time, Sherlock Holmes films are bound to appear less frequently. Some four years after the release of *A Study in Terror* there was some alarm at the news that Billy Wilder was making a Sherlock Holmes film. This concern was in no way lessened by Wilder's refusal to disclose in advance what the story of the film was to be. Wilder's many successes include those marvellous films *Sunset Boulevard* and *The Apartment*, and clearly any new film by such a master of sardonic humour was not likely to be conventional. But any fears that the Sherlock Holmes image would be damaged in some way were obviously quite unfounded. Holmes has survived too many mishandlings and debunkings to need anyone rushing to his protection.

The Private Life of Sherlock Holmes is the first Sherlock Holmes film to have been made by one of the world's major directors. Apart from the direction, it was also written by Billy Wilder, in collaboration with

I. A. L. Diamond, and so it bears Wilder's hallmark on every foot of film and every line of dialogue. Sherlock Holmes has long been an established British institution, and is an obvious target for Wilder to send up, but on this occasion it has been rightly held that Billy Wilder succumbed to the attraction of the legend, for although Wilder has his fun at innumerable moments, the film is charming and affectionate, and, at the end, extremely touching. It probes, for the first time, the vulnerability of Sherlock Holmes as a person, rather than the case-hardened reasoning machine that is the public embodiment of the great detective, and the film's title rings true. Wilder himself explained: 'I wanted to show a human being, not an abstraction. I wasn't trying to destroy the traditional character – that would be like making a film about Hitler and suddenly you discover he's Jewish. You *can't* destroy an image, only illuminate.'

The opening of the film, in which a present-day descendant of Dr Watson opens a box of unpublished cases, briskly mocks the Sherlock Holmes cult, and then we are straight back to Baker Street in the 1880s, and Holmes throwing off his cape and deerstalker – 'an improbable costume which the public now expects me to wear', and complaining to Watson about the exaggerations in his narratives that have given Holmes a public image he obviously doesn't enjoy. In no time at all they have been lured to the Russian ballet, and Sherlock Holmes is being propositioned by Petrova, the prima ballerina, who wants him to sire a child of prodigious brain for her, in return for a Stradivarius. Holmes gets himself out of this delicate situation by inferring that, like Tchaikovsky, he finds men more attractive, and has spent five very happy years living with another bachelor. During this interview Watson has been enjoying himself at a backstage party which has plentiful supplies of vodka and young ballerinas, and there is a hilarious scene where the rumour about Holmes and Watson spreads round the party and Watson finds his dancing partners have suddenly changed from girls to boys. The suggestion of homosexuality was seized on by the Press, who gave the film some unusual publicity.

This episode was intended to be one of several in a film that was originally some two and three quarter to three hours long, but in the final version to be released the other episodes had been removed, and the film moved on to the main plot of Sherlock Holmes becoming involved in helping the wife of a Belgian engineer to trace her missing husband. A menacing Mycroft Holmes summons his brother to the corridors of power and warns him not to pursue the investigation further, but Sherlock persists and travels to Scotland with Watson and Madame Valladon where they eventually find that Madame Valladon's husband has died during secret experimental trials of a British submarine. Queen Victoria refuses to launch the vessel when she learns it is a warship, and Mycroft conspires with Sherlock to reveal its whereabouts to Madame Valladon's accomplices, who steal it and perish with it. We are left in uncertainty as to how long Sherlock Holmes has known that she is really a top German spy, Ilse von Hoffmannsthal, and as she is taken away by Mycroft (to be exchanged for a British agent) Sherlock is much affected by her plight.

The final, very moving scene takes place months later, when Mycroft considerately sends Sherlock a note to tell him of an intelligence report that Ilse von Hoffmannsthal has been caught spying in Japan and executed. She had been operating there under the false name she and Sherlock Holmes had used travelling to Scotland as man and wife.

Billy Wilder's direction of this film was extraordinarily interesting, and, like the marvellous Victorian sets, so full of good things that the film deserved more than one visit. There were passing allusions to various well-known films – the train journey to Scotland (*The Thirty-Nine Steps* and *The Lady Vanishes*), the bogus married couple in the sleeping compartment (*North by North West*), the picnic by the lake (*Elvira Madigan*), the idyllic cycle ride through the countryside (*Butch Cassidy and the Sundance Kid*), Stanley Holloway as a gravedigger (the same actor in Laurence Olivier's *Hamlet*) – for those who like to spot *hommages* in a director's work.

Christopher Lee, a former Henry Baskerville *and* Sherlock Holmes, was this time Mycroft Holmes, for once a character of some significance in the plot, and although less than corpulent, excellently played.

The trouble with the Dr Watson of Colin Blakeley lay not in the acting, but in the directing. Colin Blakeley was extremely good, loyal and devoted but constantly put-upon. Billy Wilder put him through many of the scenes as if he were Jack Lemmon, in a frantic near-farcical style reminiscent of *Some Like It Hot* and *Irma La Douce*, and the over-done comedy spoiled a number of good comic scenes.

Robert Stephens, another Shakespearian actor and assistant director of the National Theatre, took on an unprecedented task in the portrayal of Sherlock Holmes as conceived by Billy Wilder, and came through it remarkably well. Wilder chose him because of his acting abilities, and also because 'he looked as if he could be hurt'. Well, his Holmes *is* hurt in a variety of ways, by a variety of people, but with no diminishing of Holmes's stature. The humanising of Sherlock Holmes is an absorbing spectacle, performed in a sensitive and stylish manner by Robert Stephens.

With the tremendous competition in the cinema from such modern upstarts as James Bond and the anti-hero school of agents, there is little likelihood of many more Sherlock Holmes films being made in the usual straightforward form; nor, it seems, is there much chance for the unusual approach, for *The Private Life of Sherlock Holmes* was not a big box-office success, and neither was *They Might Be Giants*, the film version of James Goldman's play, brilliantly directed by Antony Harvey and superbly acted by George C. Scott and Joanne Woodward, and the latest Holmes feature film to have been made.

But, with an unusual twist, it is a return to the stage that has provided the latest and most extraordinary demonstration of the popularity of Sherlock Holmes. In the autumn of 1973 the Royal Shakespeare Company decided to present, as their Christmas entertainment, a revival of William Gillette's play, *Sherlock Holmes*. It seemed an unusual choice, and a considerable gamble, but their judgement proved to be sound, and they found themselves with a huge success on their hands. So, after a gap of nearly seventy years, the Gillette play was back in the West End at the Aldwych Theatre, packing in the crowds exactly as it had done just along the street at the Lyceum in 1901, and the success was equally well deserved.

The whole production was splendid, and was carefully based on the original Gillette presentation, retaining much of his stage business. John Wood, yet another Shakespearian actor, gave us a world-weary character, alternating between bouts of langour and spasms of vigorous activity, in a highly concentrated performance of great intensity and delicate control. He was opposed by Philip Locke as Moriarty, in a thrilling depiction of great force and melodrama.

Frank Dunlop's production was not without its jokes, however, right from the opening music before the curtain rises. Low and lugubrious, played very slowly on cellos, it tantalised the memory until the curtain was up and the thick London fog rolled in from the wings, by which time one realised that it was the James Bond music. Again, the scene in Moriarty's underground office was adorned with a Mona Lisa and a Goya Duke of Wellington, the latter being a visual joke from a James Bond film. As with Gillette's production, the scene changes were made in total darkness, without a curtain drop; it was a very new thing in 1901, although commonplace enough now. At the Aldwych the scene changes were made using a big revolve and were also covered by short pieces of linking action on the apron of the stage by Victorian newsvendors, street-singers, sightseers, policemen and the like. The marvellous sets, by Carl Toms, justly received applause, and everything was carried out with obvious care and affection for the Sherlock Holmes traditions. The play remained in the repertoire of the RSC at the Aldwych Theatre until August 1974, and then paid an equally successful visit to the USA.

CHAPTER 8

'I Can Take a Joke with the Best, Mr Holmes'

Though he might be more humble, there's no police like Holmes.

E. W. Hornung

There can be no greater testimonial to the popularity and fame of Sherlock Holmes than the immeasurable number of comic imitations that have appeared over the years. Parodies, skits, take-offs, send-ups, call them what you will; Holmes has provoked examples of every type and continues to do so, particularly on television, where the many interminable comedy series are glad of Sherlock Holmes as a standard subject to be guyed.

The very name Sherlock Holmes has been a gift to those burlesquing the character. Most of the many comic and bizarre versions are easily recognisable variations from the very early 'Sherlaw Kombs' and 'Picklock Holes' to Beatle John Lennon's 'Shamrock Wolmbs and Dr Whopper'.

In 1902, *Sheerluck Jones* was not just another version of the well-known name; it was the title of a very good parody of the Gillette play then at the Lyceum Theatre. *Sheerluck Jones* or *Why D'Gillette Him Off?* was described by its authors as 'A dramatic criticism in four pages and as many headlines', and it really made great fun of the dignified Gillette, who tended to take himself and his plays very seriously.

The advertisements and programmes for the Gillette *Sherlock Holmes* carried the following SPECIAL NOTE:

As the interest of the play commences with the rising of the curtain, it is requested that the audience may be in their seats at the time announced.

The audiences for *Sheerluck Jones*, on the other hand, were warned that:

No one arriving after 10 o'clock and very few seated before that hour, can possibly understand the plot of the piece.

The burlesque enjoyed a great success, both in London and on tour.

The earliest in the field of humorous adventures also contained the very first impersonations of Sherlock Holmes and Dr Watson given in public. The occasion was one of the first English revues to take the stage; the date – November 1893. It was entitled *Under the Clock* and was written by Charles Brookfield and Seymour Hicks, both outstanding wits of their day. The piece, described in the programme as an extravaganza, took the form of a sketch which satirised Sherlock Holmes's methods of deduction. For example, to enable him to determine the nationality of an expected client, Holmes instructs Watson to place a dictionary over the door as a booby-trap. The client enters, the book falls on his head and he obligingly yells: 'Ah! Qu'est-ce que c'est? Sapristi! Goddamm!' Holmes eventually assumes a variety of disguises as he follows a suspect, and this provides the excuse for a whole series of song-and-dance items to complete the programme.

The extravaganza was not confined to guying the Sherlock Holmes stories but succeeded in satirising notable theatrical performances and plays of the day, with take-offs of Beerbohm Tree, Henry Irving, Wilson Barrett, Squire Bancroft and Mrs Patrick Campbell. Although restricted in its targets to the theatrical world, the piece must have hit the London stage with something of the impact of *That Was the Week that Was* on BBC Television.

There is a certain wry irony in the course of subsequent events. Brookfield, the irreverent mocker, was made Lord Chamberlain and had the job of censoring stage scripts and removing undesirable material.

Of course, the tremendous success of Gillette's play stimulated a number of take-offs besides *Sheerluck Jones*, especially in the British music halls, while in New York, Walter R. Seymour mimicked

Gillette's performance in a fifteen-minute travesty called *Surelock Holmes*, by Clay M. Greene, which, to judge from the reports, might have been better named 'Holmezapoppin'.

But the good parodies were few; many other skits have now disappeared without a trace, although strange examples occasionally come to light, like the all-negro show called *In Dahomey* which toured Britain in 1904, with comedians Dan Avery and Charles Hart appearing as Rarebuck Pinkerton and Shylock Homestead.

Just as Sherlock Holmes adventures were immensely popular in the earlier days of the cinema, so were films which made fun of the Holmes legend. Some were fairly cleverly observed parodies of the original stories, but the majority merely used the great name (or a distortion of the great name) as an excuse for yet another rough-and-tumble slapstick comedy.

As the great film factory of the world, Hollywood was responsible for most of these, although a few originated elsewhere. Way back in 1909, for example, Leon Gaumont produced a film shown in Germany as *Detektiv Barock Holmes und sein Hund,* and in the same year Gaumont presented in England *The Latest Triumph of Sherlock Holmes.* Made in France, it contained some shrewd digs at some of Sherlock Holmes's idiosyncrasies. It guyed his methods of creeping about the floor with a tape and magnifying glass in search of clues and showed him tracing a thief with the help of a discarded cigar. Also in 1909, in the USA, Edison was offering *Miss Sherlock Holmes.* Giving the title a feminine twist was a treatment to which the Edison Company returned in 1914 with *The Sherlock Holmes Girl.* Bliss Milford, who played the girl, was a hotel maid who unmasks a jewel thief simply by shadowing someone she thinks must be a suspicious character because there is absolutely nothing unusual about him!

In the earliest days of entertainment films in Europe every company had its tame comedian who appeared in a new escapade every week or fortnight. The screen names chosen for these clowns were indicative of the mental level that film makers attributed to their audiences. In these sophisticated times we marvel at the naïvety of such names as Foolshead, Funnicuss, Tweedledum and Wiffles, but at the time that these comic Sherlock Holmes films were being made in abundance they were all actively in the fashion. Thus we had *Moritz sieqt über*

Sherlock Holmes (1914), *Tweedledum and the Necklace* (1911), *Gontran emulates Sherlock Holmes* (1914), *Fricot als Sherlock Holmes* (1913), *Sherlock Ambrose* (1918) and so on.

The film industry certainly deserves the credit (or the opprobium) for some of the most grotesque variations on the name of Sherlock Holmes. The dreadful-sounding Burstup Homes turned up in *Burstup Homes Murder Case* and *The Case of the Missing Girl*, both in 1913. It must have been a bad year for names, because also in 1913 there was *Homlock Shermes*, and, believe it or not, that was all about Pearl, the girl detective!

Other frightful variations on the name were *Hemlock Hoax* (1910), *Padlock Bones* (1914) and *Charlie Colms* (1912). Not very much better was *Surelock Jones, Detective* (1912), a title that bears a little resemblance to *Surelock Homes*, a silent Felix the Cat cartoon (date unknown but probably early twenties). This simply dealt with the efforts of Felix to lock himself in his home away from danger, hence the title.

A pair of names that are guaranteed to make most Holmesians wince are Sherlocko and Watso, who appeared in several comedies based upon a cartoon strip, the first of which was *The Robbery at the Railroad Station* (1912). The results were extremely crude, even for early film comedy. The Imp Film Company beat them by about a month with the release of their equally corny comedy *The Flag of Distress*, which had as its famous detective – Mr Sherlocko!

An English contribution was *A Case for Sherlock Holmes* (1911), a trick film in which a sneak thief magically changed his appearance every time he was pursued. The only connection with Sherlock Holmes at all was that his name made an attractive title for the film, and this use of the correct name was frequently the only slender connection with the subject. On a number of occasions it was an excuse for one of those sickly kiddie films that film makers inflict on us so determinedly. Gaumont had a five year old child star called Bobby who appeared in *Bobby Turns Detective* in 1911. But in Germany, where Bobby was known as Fritzchen, the same film came out as *Fritzchen als Sherlock Holmes*. Pathé presented *A Midget Sherlock Holmes* in 1912, concerning 'a very small boy with beard and make-up to look like a detective'. In the USA *Baby Sherlock* (1912) showed how 'a child cleverly secures the restoration of a sum of money that has been stolen'. Prior to this came *Sherlock Holmes Junior* (1911). This was summarised as follows:

> A youngster, deciding to unravel the mystery of his father's disappearing whisky, discovers the cook drinking it and adulterates the liquor with a soporific drug, which victimizes house guests and proves instrumental in the capture of two burglars.

A very similar title, *Sherlock Junior*, was used by the great Buster Keaton in 1924 for a movie in which he is studying from a text-book on how to be a detective and manages to get himself framed for theft. Another great comedian of the screen, Larry Semon, master of the automobile gag, wrote and directed *A Villainous Villain* (1916), with Hughey Mack as Sherlock Oomph, the great detective whose sweetheart is stolen by a master crook.

But for a sustained attack on anyone's dignity there was no one to approach the ebullient, self-styled King of Comedy – Mack Sennett himself. Sennett believed that there is nothing that deflates pomposity and authority like a kick in the pants, and that is what happened to Sherlock Holmes on the many occasions that Sennett let fly.

It all began in 1911 at the Biograph studios in New York, where the legendary D. W. Griffith was turning out scores of good quality dramas acted by the Gish sisters, Mary Pickford and all the other now-historic players, while Mack Sennett was appearing in, and sometimes directing, some of the Biograph comedies. Sennett and Fred Mace appeared as two comic detectives decked out in Sherlock Holmes attire in a split-reel comedy entitled *$500.00 Reward*. As may be expected, the sequence of slapstick events ended up with the Sleuths, as they came to be known, getting at cross purposes with the police, whom they were aiming to assist. The success of this comedy brought forth an early sequel called *Trailing the Counterfeiter*, followed by three more Sleuths titles, all within eight months.

In all these films the Sleuths attempted in various ways to emulate the methods of Sherlock Holmes, invariably with disastrous results. Their well-meant efforts at detection usually ended in fights, chases and general destruction of property. Sennett had no time for subtleties. His was the knock-down drag-out type of slapstick made at a furious pace, and his comedies were enormously popular. He particularly wanted to make some films with comic policemen but Griffith would have none of it.

When Mack Sennett left Biograph in 1912 to found the legendary Keystone Studio, he took with him most of the Biograph comedy team. Fred Mace had already left Biograph for another company, but when Keystone moved to California he rejoined Sennett, and in no time at all the Sleuths were, in the words of their next title, *At It Again*. That was in November 1912, and in the following six months the Sleuths appeared in five more films. They also made a personal appearance in costume as part of the Pasadena Tournament of Roses in January 1913. Not content with riding in the florally decorated automobile that was Keystone's entry in the parade (and which incidentally won second prize), they spent a lot of time trying to evade Mabel Normand, who was frantically trying to catch up with the Keystone car, having been locked in her dressing-room to keep her away. Another Keystone comedian, Ford Sterling, had been planted in the crowd to add to the confusion among police and spectators. The astute Mack Sennett had cameramen on hand to film all the high jinks, and the results were quickly released as another Keystone comedy, *The Sleuths at the Floral Parade*.

The last Sleuths film was *Their First Execution* and had only Sennett in it. It was literally the end of the Sleuths. Only a month earlier Keystone had released a comedy with a significant title – *The Bangville Police*, which was effectively the forerunner of that fantastic creation, the Keystone Kops. Once Sennett was in charge, and had established his new studio, he was able to explore the comic possibilities of policemen, and after that the Sleuths stood no chance of surviving. In any case, Fred Mace had already left Sennett to go to the Majestic Company, and *he* made one more film in Sleuth garb, *The Tongue Mark*, before that short-lived company folded up.

At a time when many film skits on Sherlock Holmes were being made in the course of a vast output of comedy films, the Sleuths lasted a remarkably long while. They were amazingly popular in an era when people were much more able to laugh at themselves; when the fun makers didn't take themselves seriously either. 'We made funny pictures as fast as we could for money,' said Mack Sennett.

CHAPTER 9

'Which of You Is Holmes?'

Almost anybody can play Hamlet, and nearly everybody does; but there are only a few actors on earth, one is convinced, capable of playing Sherlock Holmes. Those few not only *play* the part; they *look* and *are* the part.

Vincent Starrett

For well over eighty years Sherlock Holmes has enjoyed a popularity that has made him the most widely known character in all the world's fiction, and he continues in this popularity decade after decade. Why is this so?

The well-known detective-story writer Rex Stout has suggested an answer that comes closest to explaining the phenomenon, namely that Sherlock Holmes is the embodiment of man's dearest and most stubborn conceit: that he is the *reasoning animal*, homo sapiens. As Rex Stout goes on to say: 'Our aspiration to put our reason in control of our instincts and emotions is so deep and intense that we constantly pretend we are doing so. We almost never are, but Sherlock Holmes always is.'

So we identify with Holmes, and today that means we are identifying with a person of the late-Victorian era, of a stable and orderly way of life, of modes and manners and integrity that all seem to belong to an historic past. Sherlock Holmes is no longer merely out-of-date, as in the 1930s and 1940s when all the films were modernised; he belongs to a period that is now recognised as uniquely settled and serene, and we tend to envy the inhabitants of it.

Towards the end of his life Sir Arthur Conan Doyle said, 'The impression that Holmes was a real person of flesh and blood may have been intensified by his frequent appearances upon the stage.' I have always considered that to be an extremely grudging admission, for if this book succeeds in anything at all it demonstrates how all the various dramatisations have advanced the renown of an already celebrated creation.

Conversely, the very name is sufficient to sell the drama – 'Sherlock Holmes in A STUDY IN TERROR' ran the advertisements for that particular film – which is perhaps just as well, for we have moved from the custom of star performances towards the concept of ensemble playing, as demonstrated by the adventures featuring Sherlock Holmes as played by John Neville, Robert Stephens and John Wood. Although their portrayals have been immensely satisfying, they will never become typed as Sherlock Holmes in the way that the four really outstanding impersonators did.

It was the lot of William Gillette, Eille Norwood, Arthur Wontner and Basil Rathbone to become so closely identified with the famous character they regularly portrayed that occasionally their private lives were rendered uncomfortable in the extreme. Like Conan Doyle, they wished at times to throw off Holmes altogether, for they could hardly walk down the street without being recognised and accosted as Sherlock Holmes.

Such marked association of character with actor was unusual, and was experienced by very few performers in the days before actors became so typed by television. People did not, for example, point out Sir John Gielgud or Sir Laurence Olivier in the street and say 'There's Hamlet.' The close resemblance of the great portrayers of Holmes to the accepted appearance of the character has contributed to this, but their successes in the interpretation of the role were due to much more than their physical appearance.

An author needs no interpreter to bring his creation before the public. The dramatist, on the other hand, is obliged to have his work performed if it is to make its full impact, and the performances may or may not be successful in carrying out the dramatist's intentions. It is often difficult to determine where the responsibility for the result lies. Some considerable dramatisations have been utter failures when acted by ill-trained and uninterested players, while much poor material has been made to appear far better than it really is by superlative actors.

The stage and screen adventures of Sherlock Holmes mostly fall into the second category, and the four actors mentioned above have all been responsible for the uplifting of mediocre material by sheer acting ability. They were all trained in a hard school of stage experience, and in their films they quite overshadowed the lesser players of the screen, beside whom their behaviour was no natural and convincing that they did not appear to be acting at all. In fact they *became* Sherlock Holmes, and so complete was their loss of personal identity that it is as Sherlock Holmes that they are remembered by the public, long after their other roles, and sometimes even their names, have been forgotten. Moreover, to a considerable degree the very acting careers of these players was influenced by their connections with Sherlock Holmes. After playing this role none of them ever seemed to achieve another really great part.

Even William Gillette came to wish he could rid himself of Holmes. In a letter to Charles Frohman in 1905 he said, 'I want to make money on "Holmes" quick – so as to be *through with it*!!' Could he have stood it, had he known there were another twenty-seven years to go?

Basil Rathbone was bitterly forthright about it:

> Eventually my identification with the character of Sherlock Holmes so completely overwhelmed me that when I returned to New York in 1945 theatre producers would not touch me at the end of a large pole! Agreeing that I would be well cast in several plays, they all decided against me, saying no audience, whatever part I played and how ever well I played it, could ever think of me except as Sherlock Holmes! . . . You see, when you *become* the character you portray it's the end of your career as an actor.

The many other actors who have tackled this Everest of a role must not be forgotten; while never achieving the same degree of identification, they have given enjoyment and entertainment to millions. Today, with the medium of television in our very homes, this can mean millions all at once; and perhaps because of this we shall look in vain for another great Sherlock Holmes on the small screen, for the one thing that television cannot by its very location create for us is the glamour which is to be found in the cinema and the theatre, where the sense of distance and isolation from the source of the action makes it all so much larger than life.

Sherlock Holmes, the unique character created by Conan Doyle, has that glamour, that presence, that air of always being somebody; yet at times he is human enough to be vain, prejudiced, intolerant and occasionally fallible. In a period when the gifted amateur detective has largely been displaced by the regular police and officially sponsored investigators, Sherlock Holmes alone goes on and on, seemingly forever. Even though, in Billy Wilder's film, Holmes is matched against a large government agency and loses, we see that it is human frailty that has really defeated him, and our sentiments are with Sherlock rather than Mycroft, who epitomises 'the system'.

In exercising their sometimes severe criticism of the various dramatisations of Sherlock Holmes, some writers are apt to forget that a producer's main purpose is to make his entertainment a success, rather than a faithful copy of the original, which is at best a secondary consideration and in some cases is scarcely thought of at all. But throughout all the performances of all the dramatisations the magic of Sherlock Holmes usually manages to shine through somewhere, despite adaptations and impersonations that have not always appealed to us. In 1901 the dramatic critic of *The Daily Telegraph* wrote, 'We must not hide from ourselves the fact that Sherlock Holmes, like many another figure in fiction, is more impressive in imagination than in the flesh.' A truism, of course, but very coldly stated. Many of us who have been thrilled by some of the dramatised adventures of the great detective would prefer to express ourselves much more warmly, as did Dr Mortimer in the final scene of *The Hound of the Baskervilles* (1939):

Mr. Holmes, we've admired you in the past, as does every Englishman. Your record as our greatest detective is known throughout the world, but this – seeing how you work, knowing that there is in England such a man as you – gives us all a sense of safety and security.

Catalogue of Performances

There are a good many other points of detail which will, no
doubt, come to light in good time.

His Last Bow

This catalogue of all the known dramatic productions featuring Sherlock
Holmes has been made as comprehensive as is reasonably possible, but
details of additions and corrections will be welcomed. It is arranged in
chronological lists of plays, films, radio plays, television plays and
records.

Stage Presentations of Sherlock Holmes

UNDER THE CLOCK 1893
An extravaganza in one act by C. H. E. Brookfield and Seymour Hicks. Music by Edward Jones.
Produced at the Royal Court Theatre, London, 25 Nov 1893 for 92 performances.
Sherlock Holmes: C. H. E. Brookfield. Dr Watson: Seymour Hicks.

SHERLOCK HOLMES 1894
A play in five acts by Charles Rogers.
First produced at the Theatre Royal, Glasgow, 28 May 1894 for one week. Given by Cordyce & Hamund's Company.
(Copyright performance given at the Theatre Royal, Hanley, 15 Dec 1893 under the title *Sherlock Holmes, Private Detective*.)
Sherlock Holmes: John Webb. Dr James Watson: St John Hamund. Wilton Hursher: Arthur Lyle. Billy: Kenyon Lyle. Mrs Watson: Phyllis Manners. Ruby Hursher: Edith Lewis. Lily: Cissy Sephton.
Toured extensively until at least Apr 1902; also with Henry S. Dacre as Sherlock Holmes.

> An application was made to Mr. Justice Joyce on Thursday, (5th September) to restrain the use of the title *Sherlock Holmes* by Mr. William Gillette for the play which is to be produced at the Lyceum. The application was made by Mr. Frank Rothsay, as assignee from the executors of the late Mr. Charles Rogers . . . The Lyceum management contended that their play would not injure the other drama, and Mr. Justice Joyce refused the injunction.
>
> *The Era* (7 Sept 1901)

BRANSBY WILLIAMS 1898
Character sketches from the classics, including Sherlock Holmes. 'Sherlock Holmes was a great success, as I gave three changes in the one character.'

First performed at the London Pavilion, 26 Sept 1898, and repeated there in May 1902.

SHERLOCK HOLMES 1899

A drama in four acts by Arthur Conan Doyle and William Gillette.
(Copyright performance given at the Duke of York's Theatre, London, 12 June 1899.)
(1) First produced at the Star Theatre, Buffalo, 23 Oct 1899 for three nights.
(2) Produced in Syracuse for one night and Rochester for one night during the week commencing 30 Oct 1899.
(3) Produced at the Garrick Theatre, New York, 6 Nov 1899 for 236 performances, closing on 16 June 1900.
Sherlock Holmes: William Gillette. Dr Watson: Bruce McRae. Professor Moriarty: George Wessells.
(4) Second American production, first given at the Montauk Theatre, Brooklyn, 8 Oct 1900, for two weeks, and toured in USA until 30 March 1901. Sherlock Holmes: William Gillette
(5) First produced in England at the Shakespeare Theatre, Liverpool, 2 Sept 1901 for one week.
(6) Produced at the Lyceum Theatre, London, 9 Sept 1901 for 216 performances, closing on 11 Apr 1902. Gillette and company then toured Great Britain for eight weeks before returning to USA.
Sherlock Holmes: William Gillette. Dr Watson: Percy Lyndal. Professor Moriarty: W. L. Abingdon. Billy: Henry McArdle. Alice Faulkner: Maude Fealy.
(7) Third American production in Springfield, Massachusetts, 17 Oct 1902. Sherlock Holmes: William Gillette.
Performed in New York, Washington and Chicago.
(8) Fourth American production at the Empire Theatre, New York City, 6 March 1905 for 56 performances. Sherlock Holmes: William Gillette.
(9) Second British production at the Duke of York's Theatre, London, 17 Oct 1905 for 48 performances.
Sherlock Holmes: William Gillette. Dr Watson: Kenneth Rivington. Professor Moriarty: George Sumner. Sidney Prince: Quinton McPherson. Billy: Charles Chaplin. Alice Faulkner: Marie Doro.
(10) Fifth American production at the Opera House, Chicago, 15 Oct 1906. Sherlock Holmes: William Gillette.
(11) Sixth American production at the Empire Theatre, New York City, 5 Dec 1910. Sherlock Holmes: William Gillette.
(12) Seventh American production at the Empire Theatre, New York City, 8 Oct 1915, and later at the Blackstone Theatre, Chicago. Sherlock Holmes: William Gillette.
(13) Eighth American production in Philadelphia, 8 Jan 1923, and later at the National Theatre, Washington. Sherlock Holmes: William Gillette.

(14) Ninth American production at the Cosmopolitan Theatre, New York City, 20 Feb 1928. Sherlock Holmes: Robert Warwick.

(15) Tenth American production – William Gillette's Farewell Tour. Opened in Springfield, Massachusetts, 15 Nov 1929; the final performance appears to have been 19 March 1932, at the Playhouse, Wilmington, Delaware.

Sherlock Holmes: William Gillette. Dr Watson: Wallis Clark. Professor Moriarty: John Miltern. Sidney Prince: William Postance.

(16) Third British production by the Royal Shakespeare Company at the Aldwych Theatre, London, 1 Jan 1974 for 106 performances.

Directed by Frank Dunlop.

Sherlock Holmes: John Wood. Dr Watson: Tim Pigott-Smith. Madge Larrabee: Barbara Leigh-Hunt. John Forman: Harry Towb. James Larrabee: Nicholas Selby. Terese: Madeline Bellamy. Sidney Prince: Trevor Peacock. Alice Faulkner: Mary Rutherford. Professor Moriarty: Philip Locke. John: Paul Gaynon. Alfred Bassick: Martin Milman. Billy: Sean Clarke.

(17) British provincial and touring company productions:

Chas Frohman's North Company, March 1902–June 1905. Sherlock Holmes: H. A. Saintsbury.

Chas Frohman's South Company, March 1902–May 1904. Sherlock Holmes: Julian Royce.

Chas Frohman's Midland Company, Jan 1904–May 1905. Sherlock Holmes: Kenneth Rivington.

Ben Greet's Touring Companies, two companies touring from 26 Dec 1901, with various actors as Sherlock Holmes, including T. A. Shannon, Henry S. Dacre, J. S. Crawley, Fred Sargent and Ernest Bliss.

Harry Yorke's Company, Aug 1905–June 1906, with H. Lawrence Leyton and Henry Renouf as Sherlock Holmes.

H. Hamilton Stewart's Company, Aug 1906–Dec 1917. Sherlock Holmes: H. Hamilton Stewart.

Leo Trood's Company, Feb 1919–Nov 1923, with various actors as Sherlock Holmes, including Harold Holland, Laurence Carter, Leonard Tremayne and Leo Trood.

Hamilton Deane's Company, c1923–Jan 1932. (The play carried in the repertoire with several other plays.) Sherlock Holmes: Hamilton Deane. Sid Prince: Jack Howarth. Billy: Sydney Howarth.

A Birmingham Repertory Company, 21 June 1926 at the Alexandria Theatre, Birmingham.

Sherlock Holmes: John Blake. Dr Watson: Gwyn Nichols.

Cecil Barth's Company, 10 June–28 Sept 1929.

Sherlock Holmes: H. A. Saintsbury. Dr Watson: George E. Pearson. Professor Moriarty: Quinton McPherson.

The Northampton Repertory Players, 21–26 Apr 1930 at the Repertory Theatre, Northampton.

Sherlock Holmes: Noel Howlett. Dr Watson: William Aldous.

The Birmingham Repertory Theatre, 4–29 March 1952.
Sherlock Holmes: Alfred Burke. Dr Watson: Paul Daneman. Professor Moriarty: Alan Bridges.
(18) Overseas productions:
Denmark
Danish version by Walter Christmas, first given at the Folketeatret, Copenhagen, 26 Dec 1901.
Sherlock Holmes: Dorph-Peterson. Professor Moriarty: Emil Helsengreen.
Produced at the Aarhus Teater, Aarhus, 1902. Sherlock Holmes: Vilhelm Birch.
Produced at the Aalborg Teater, Aalborg, 1902. Sherlock Holmes: Otto Lagoni.
Revived at the Folketeatret, Copenhagen, 26 Apr 1908. Sherlock Holmes: Albrecht Schmidt. Professor Moriarty: Emil Helsengreen.
Produced at the Sonderbros Teater, Copenhagen, 26 Sept 1915. Sherlock Holmes: Herman Florents. Professor Moriarty: Max Ibenfeldt.
Holland
Grand Theatre, Amsterdam, 11 Jan 1902.
Sherlock Holmes: Marcel Myin. Dr Watson: S. Frank. Professor Moriarty: Aug T. C. Kiehl.
Rika Hopper Theater, Amsterdam, 24 Aug 1930.
Sherlock Holmes: Eduard Verkade. Doktor Watson: Hans van Meerten. Madge Larrabee: Rika Hopper. Professor Moriarty: Albert van Dalsum.
Russia
Translation by Countess Bella. The Imperial Theatre, St Petersburg, 1 March 1902.
Sweden
Translation of Walter Christmas's Danish version.
Teatern i Folkets Hus, Stockholm, 5 Apr 1902.
Sherlock Holmes: Hr Bergendorff. Professor Moriarty: Hr Lagerman.
Folkteatern, Stockholm, 21 Apr 1902.
Sherlock Holmes: Hr Bergvall. Professor Moriarty: Hr Strandberg.
Svenska Teatern, Stockholm, 24 Apr 1902.
Sherlock Holmes: Knut Nyblom. Dr Watson: Hr Barcklind. Professor Moriarty: Justus Hagman.
Folkteatern, Gothenburg, 28 Oct 1902.
Sherlock Holmes: Emil Ljungqvist. Dr Wattson [*sic*] Alfred Anderson.
Stora Teatern, Gothenburg, 25 March 1903. Hugo Ronnblad's company.
Malmo Teater, Malmo, 19 March 1905.
Sherlock Holmes: Hugo Ronnblad. Professor Moriarty: Victor Sjöstrom.
First translation direct into Swedish, by Harald Thornberg: Helsingborgs Teater, Halsingborg, 26 Jan 1906.
Sherlock Holmes: Hugo Ronnblad. Professor Moriarty: Eric Zachrison.
Stora Teatern, Gothenburg, 1 Dec 1908.
Sherlock Holmes: Hugo Ronnblad. Dr Watson: Alfred Andersson. Professor Moriarty: Karl Borin.

Helsingborgs Stads Teater, Halsingborg, 20 March 1910.
Sherlock Holmes: Hugo Ronnblad. Professor Moriarty: Karl Borin.
Hippodromens Teater, Malmo, 17 Dec 1911.
Sherlock Holmes: Hugo Ronnblad. Professor Moriarty: Hr Fischer.
Ostermalmsteatern, Stockholm, 15 March 1913.
Sherlock Holmes: William Larsson.
Folkteatern, Gothenburg, 5 Apr 1913.
Sherlock Holmes: Hugo Ronnblad. Professor Moriarty: Olof Hillberg.
Germany
Translation by Albert Bozenhard.
Theatre (?), 19 Oct 1906 (First production ?)
Sherlok [*sic*] Holmes: Franz Scharwenka. Dr Watson: Franz Schneider.
Professor Moriarty: George Braatz.
Sherlock Holmes published by Samuel French Ltd (London, 1922).
Revised by William Gillette and published by Doubleday, Doran & Co (New York, 1935).
Published by Blakiston (New York, 1946) in *Famous Plays of Crime and Detection.*

THE BANK OF ENGLAND 1900
A drama in four acts by Max Goldberg.
First produced at the Shakespeare Theatre, Clapham, 26 Nov 1900.
Sherlock Holmes: John F. Preston.
Subsequently toured British provinces until at least 1906 with various actors as Sherlock Holmes, including St John Beecher, Hubert S. Chambers and Charles H. Lester.
First produced in USA at the Grand Theatre, New York, 15 Feb 1904, by the Boyle Stock Company.
Sherlock Holmes: Eugene Moore.

SHERLOCK HOLMES, DETECTIVE or THE SIGN OF THE FOUR
1901
A melodrama in four acts by John Arthur Fraser.
First produced at Hopkins' Theater, Chicago, 5 May 1901 for 4 performances.
Sherlock Holmes: Richard Butler. Dr Watson: Carl Smith Seerle.
Charles Frohman had a contract with Conan Doyle and William Gillette for the production rights to Gillette's *Sherlock Holmes* for five years, commencing 7 Dec 1898. On 10 May 1901 the Circuit Court of Chicago granted an injunction against the performing of *Sherlock Holmes, Detective,* and the Hopkins Amusement Company was required to pay Charles Frohman $1,000.

SHEERLUCK JONES or WHY D'GILLETTE HIM OFF? 1901
A burlesque on William Gillette's play *Sherlock Holmes* by Malcolm Watson and Edward La Serre; described as 'a dramatic criticism in four paras and as many headlines'.

First produced at Terry's Theatre in the Strand, London, 12 Oct 1901.
Sheerluck Jones: Clarence Blakiston. Dr Rotson: Carter Pickford.

> The Management desires to call the special attention of the audience to the novel light effects. For permission to reproduce these in the family circle by the method of rapidly opening and closing the eyes, application to be made to the Acting Manager.
>
> The light motives in the orchestra provided by Mr. Brigata Buccalossi. Properties by their respective owners.
>
> The costumes more by accident than design.
>
> As the orchestra is only able to play one tune in the dark, the indulgence of the public is requested should any similarity be detected in the musical finales to the various paragraphs.

Toured in the British provinces in 1902.

AN ADVENTURE IN THE LIFE OF SHERLOCK HOLMES   1902

A sketch in two episodes by John Lawson.
First produced at the Paragon Music Hall, Mile End Road, London, 6 Jan 1902, and subsequently at other music halls.
Sherlock Holmes: John Lawson. Baron de Denmar: E. S. Vincent. Sylvester Valmore: Mrs John Lawson.
Rewritten by John Lawson as 'an episode in three scenes'. First produced in this form at the Theatre Royal, Garston, 8 May 1902.
Sherlock Holmes: W. R. Perceval. Baron de Denmar: Seddon Ennis. Sylvester Valmore: Nellie Eglin.

THE GREAT DETECTIVE   1902

A dramatic sketch in three scenes by Roy Redgrave.
First produced at Sadler's Wells, 13 Jan 1902.
(Copyright performance at the Public Hall, Dorking, 10 Jan 1902.)
Sherlock Holmes: Roy Redgrave. Gilbert Ainslie: Frank Carlile. The Professor: T. W. Ford. Bulger: Edwin Bennett. Arthur Westwood: Annie Lynne. Kate Westwood: Louisa Peach.

> That wonderfully astute detective Sherlock Holmes has become a favourite theatrical character. Not only has he taken possession of the Lyceum stage, but he forms the central figure of a sketch which has been produced at Sadler's Wells this week . . . The gang of thieves has for its leader Gilbert Ainslie, who reckons much upon having in his power Arthur Westwood, a young bank clerk. Sherlock Holmes, who has received some information as to the intended robbery, assumes the character of an old Indian military officer, and, pretending he has a grudge against the bank officials, obtains admittance to Ainslie's country house and expresses his willingness to co-operate in any plan for robbing the bank. Here comes Kate Westwood, anxious concerning her brother Arthur. Pretending that her motor car broke down as she was passing, she gains admission, and when left alone with her brother begs him to quit this company of dangerous scoundrels.

The detective, who has been lying covered up on the couch, suddenly bestirs himself and assures brother and sister that they may count on his assistance . . . The supposed Colonel beats a retreat, only to return cleverly disguised, first as an old man who is in search of a lost pet dog, and next as an excitable Frenchman who bears out Kate's story respecting the motor accident . . .

Arthur Westwood is murdered by the leader of the gang and the dead body is enveloped in a wrapper and secured with rope; but Holmes again appears and, in the absence of the gang takes the place of the corpse in the covering. The 'remains' are conveyed to the cellars; then the detective's trick is discovered, and a member of the gang who has suffered imprisonment through Holmes, gloats over his impending death, but in the nick of time Kate Westwood releases him and after a struggle the members of the gang are secured. Mr. Roy Redgrave appears as the detective, and his quick changes are very smartly worked. A clever and experienced young actor, Mr. Redgrave gives a distinct individuality to each character.

The Era (18 Jan 1902)

SHERLOCK HOLMES   1902
A music-hall sketch by H. Leslie Bell.
First produced at the Palace Music Hall, Tottenham, 27 Jan 1902.
(Copyright performance 20 Jan 1902.)

SURELOCK HOLMES   1902
A vaudeville travesty by Clay M. Greene.
First produced at Proctor's 5th Avenue Theater, New York, 12 Jan 1902 for one week. Then at Proctor's 125th Street Theater, 19 Jan for one week; Proctor's 58th Street Theater, 26 Jan for one week; Proctor's 23rd Street Theater, 9 Feb for one week.
Performed by Proctor's Stock Company.
Surelock Holmes: Walter R. Seymour.

In *Surelock Holmes* . . . the deductions of the famous detective are carried to absurd extremes, and the incidents of the Gas Chamber scene are distorted in ways that make for laughter. Mr. Gillette is imitated rather than carica- tured by Walter R. Seymour, and the other characters of the drama are more or less misrepresented by the members of the Proctor stock com- pany. The leading man insists on holding the centre of the stage, and the leading woman seeks in vain to bask in the limelight. One of the villains darkens the scene by blowing out the footlights, and when the operations of the gang demand perfect silence the stage becomes a pandemonium.

The Era (1 Feb 1902)

(SHERLOCK HOLMES)   1902
A music-hall sketch by William Felton.
Produced at the Eastern Empire, Bow, March 1902.
Sherlock Holmes: William Felton.

CHARLES CONWAY 1902
Quick-change artiste and impersonator. In 1902 appearing as Wilson Barrett in *The Sign of the Cross* and as William Gillette in *Sherlock Holmes*.

THE SIGN OF THE FOUR 1903
A drama in four acts by Charles P. Rice.
First produced at the West End Theatre, New York, 9 Nov 1903 for 8 performances.
Sherlock Holmes: Walter Edwards. Dr Watson: Joseph Rawley. Inspector Athelney Jones: Van Kenzie. Jonathan Small: Franklin Tucker. Wiggins: Robert Lothian. Tonga: James Byrnes. Major Sholto: Leonard Hoyt. Lal Chowdar: William Sheetz. Mordicai Smith: George Willard. Jim Smith: William Davis. Mary Morston: Mabel Hazlett. Mrs Sholto: Georgine Braddon. Mrs Hudson: Mrs Franklin Tucker. Bessie: Agnes Porter. Mrs Smith: Jessie Barnes.
Toured the USA extensively at least until 1912.

THE PAINFUL PREDICAMENT OF SHERLOCK HOLMES 1905
An episode in one act by William Gillette.
First performed at a benefit at the Metropolitan Opera House, New York, 23 March, 1905, as *The Frightful Predicament of Sherlock Holmes*.
Sherlock Holmes: William Gillette. Billy: Henry McArdle. Miss Gwendolyn Cobb: Ethel Barrymore.
Performed at the Criterion Theater, New York, 14 Apr 1905, as *The Harrowing Predicament of Sherlock Holmes*.
First produced in England at the Duke of York's Theatre, London, 3 Oct 1905–14 Oct 1905, as a curtain-raiser to *Clarice*.
Sherlock Holmes: William Gillette. Billy: Charles Chaplin. Miss Gwendolyn Cobb: Irene Vanbrugh.
Published by Ben Abramson (Chicago, 1955).

SHERLOCK HOLMES 1905
A play by Fr von Schontau.

THE HEART OF LONDON 1906 (?)
Author unknown.
Performed at the Theatre Royal, Goole, 12 March 1906, by James Stevens' Company.
Sherlock Holmes: C. York. Dr Watson: J. Hart. Jim: J. Stephens. Bashford: T. G. Davies. Kate: M. L. Cluer. Liza: L. Victor. Mary: A. L. Earle.

SHERLOCK HOLMES 1906
A drama in four acts by Ferdinand Bonn.
First produced at the Berliner Theatre, Berlin, 2 July 1906 for 239 performances.

Sherlock Holmes: Ferdinand Bonn. Lady Katogan: Maria Bonn. Doktor Mors: Magnus Stift. Inspektor Knox: Ernst Bluziger. Inspektor Smallweed: Hermann Picka. Forbs: Paul Donner.
Published by the Philipp Reclam Verlag (Leipzig, 1906).

DER HUND VON BASKERVILLE 1907
A drama in four acts by Ferdinand Bonn.
First produced at the Berliner Theatre, Berlin, 17 Jan 1907 for 112 performances.
Sherlock Holmes: Ferdinand Bonn.
Produced at the Frederiksberg Teater, Copenhagen, in 1908.
Sherlock Holmes: Emil Wulff. Stapleton: Carl Alstrup.
Published by the Philipp Reclam Verlag (Leipzig, 1907).

A NIGHT WITH THE STARS 1907
A musical comedy hotch-potch in two scenes by Max Goldberg.
First performed at the Scala Theatre, London, 11 Feb 1907.
Sherlock Holmes: Carl Lynn.
The author provided in his work, which was in the main the music-hall scene from his play *Secrets*, the requisite vehicle for the interpolation of every phase of a music-hall programme. The show was presented in opposition to the music-hall proprietors during the so-called Music Hall War, when variety artistes, musicians and stage-hands were on strike against oppressive contract conditions. The author, Max Goldberg (John F. Preston), had earlier written *The Bank of England* (see p 123).

SHERLOCK HOLMES 1907
A drama in three acts by L. Ottomeyer.

SHERLOCK HOLMES 1907
A farce by P. Rahnheld.

SHERLOCK HOLMES IN GEBIRGE (Sherlock Holmes in the Mountains) 1907
A drama in three acts by Frau Hartl-Mitius.
Produced at the New Royal Theatre, Berlin, 11 Oct 1907.

SHERLOCK HOLMES 1907
A drama in five acts by Pierre Decourcelle, after the original of Sir Arthur Conan Doyle and William Gillette.
First produced at the Theatre Antoine, Paris, 20 Dec 1907, for 335 performances.
Sherlock Holmes: Firmin Gémier. Professor Moriarty: Harry Baur. Docteur Watson: Saillard. Murray-Orlebar: Charlier. John Alfred Napoleon Bribb: R. Terrier. Billy: P. Laurent.
Revived at the Theatre Antoine, Paris, March 1909, for 18 performances.

Sherlock Holmes: Firmin Gémier.
Revived at the Theatre National Ambulant, Paris, May 1912.
Sherlock Holmes: Firmin Gémier.
Revived at the Theatre Ambigu, Paris, 22 Oct 1915.
Sherlock Holmes: Harry Baur.
The play was published in the monthly magazine *Je Sais Tout*, in the issues for Feb–Apr 1908; also published by Pierre Lafitte (Paris, 1908).

HOLMES Y RAFLES (Holmes versus Raffles)   1908
Melodrama in five acts by Gonzalo Jover and Emilio Gonzalez del Castillo.
Produced at the Teatro Martin, Madrid, 15 June 1908.
Published by Sociedad de Autores Espagnoles (Madrid, 1908).

LA GARRA DE HOLMES (The Clutch of Holmes)   1908
The second part of *Holmes y Rafles*.
Melodrama in five scenes by Gonzalo Jover and Emilio Gonzalez del Castillo.
Produced at the Teatro Martin, Madrid, 15 June 1908, immediately following the first part.
Published by Sociedad de Autores Espagnoles (Madrid, 1908).

SHERLOCK HOLMES   1908
A drama by K. Weiss.

LA CAPTURA DE RAFFLES, O EL TRIUNFO DE SHERLOCK HOLMES (The Capture of Raffles, or The Triumph of Sherlock Holmes) 1908
A drama in a prologue and five acts by Luis Milla and G. X. Roura.
First produced at the Teatro Moderno, Barcelona, 29 Nov 1908.
Sherlok [*sic*] Holmes: Sr Olivar. Dr Walton: Sr Salom. Raffles: Sr Roura. Buck: Sr Milla.
Published by Sociedad de Autores Espagnoles (Madrid, 1912).

NADIE MAS FUERTE QUE SHERLOCK HOLMES (Nobody Stronger than Sherlock Holmes)   1909
A drama in six acts by Luis Milla and Guillermo X. Roura. The second part of *La Captura de Raffles*, based on Maurice Leblanc's *Arsène Lupin contre Herlock Sholmes*.
First produced at the Teatro Arnau, Barcelona, 27 Feb 1909.
Sherlock Holmes: Sr Guixer. Raffles: Sr Saumell.
Published by Sociedad de Autores Espagnoles (Madrid, 1913).

A STUDY IN SCARLET   1909
A drama in (?) acts by Paul Sarauw.
Produced at the Frederiksberg Teater, Copenhagen, 1909.

Sherlock Holmes: Carl Alstrup. Jefferson Hope: Robert Schmidt.

THE SPECKLED BAND 1910
An adventure in three acts by Arthur Conan Doyle.
First produced at the Adelphi Theatre in the Strand, London, 4 June 1910 for
169 performances (transferred to the Globe Theatre, 8 Aug 1910).
Sherlock Holmes: H. A. Saintsbury. Dr Watson: Claude King. Billy: Cecil F.
Lowrie. Dr Grimesby Rylott: Lyn Harding. Enid Stonor: Christine Silver.
Mr Armitage: Spencer Trevor.
Saintsbury reached his thousandth performance as Holmes on 30 July 1910, on
which occasion Conan Doyle presented him with a gold cigarette case, suitably
inscribed in facsimile of Doyle's handwriting.
First produced in USA at the Garrick Theater, New York, 21 Nov 1910 for
32 performances.
Sherlock Holmes: Charles Millward. Dr Watson: Ivo Dawson. Dr Grimesby
Rylott: Edwin Stevens. Enid Stonor: Irene Fenwick. Mr Armitage: Ben Field.
Revived at the Strand Theatre, London, 6 Feb 1911 for 21 performances.
Sherlock Holmes: O. P. Heggie. Dr Rylott: Lyn Harding. Enid Stonor:
Christine Silver.
Third British production at the St James's Theatre, London, 22 Sept 1921 for
124 performances (transferred to the Royalty Theatre, 26 Dec 1921).
Sherlock Holmes: H. A. Saintsbury. Dr Watson: Kenneth Rivington. Dr
Grimesby Rylott: Lyn Harding. Billy: Victor Pierpoint. Enid Stonor: Mary
Merrall.
British provincial and touring company productions:
Arthur Hardy's South Company, Sept 1910–(?)1912 with O. P. Heggie,
Grendon Bentley, and E. Vassal Vaughan as Sherlock Holmes.
Arthur Hardy's North Company, July 1910–cSept 1914 with Julian Royce,
H. A. Saintsbury, A. Corney Grain, Grendon Bentley, Herbert Bradford, and
Sydney Bland as Sherlock Holmes.
Horsfield & Woodward's Company, Dec 1914–Oct 1915 with Charles York,
R. Goodyer-Kettley, and Herbert Stanton as Sherlock Holmes.
C. W. Somerset's Company, Nov 1915–May 1916 with H. A. Young as
Sherlock Holmes.
Harold V. Neilson's Company, 1917 with Harold V. Neilson as Sherlock
Holmes.
The London Players, cFeb–Oct 1922 with Henry Oscar, and Robert Gilbert
as Sherlock Holmes.
Lister & Barclay's Company, cApr–Sept 1923 with Rupert Lister as Sherlock
Holmes.
Produced at the Library Theatre, Manchester, 22 Sept–10 Oct 1970.
Sherlock Holmes: Alan Moore. Dr Watson: Michael Keating. Dr Roylott:
Mike Savage. Mr Armitage: Ian McDiarmid.
Produced at Stora Teatern, Gothenberg, 21 Oct 1912 for 8 performances.

Adapted and produced by Einar Froberg.
Sherlock Holmes: Einar Froberg. Dr Watson: Henric Ljungberg. Dr Roylott: Richard Lund.
Toured in USA by the Liebler Company 1914.
Sherlock Holmes: H. Cooper Cliffe. Dr Watson: David Proctor. Dr Rylott: Lyn Harding.
Produced at Théâtre Albert 1er, Paris, summer 1925, by Edward Stirling's company.
Sherlock Holmes: Edward Stirling. Dr Watson: Charles Bennet.
Published by Samuel French Ltd (London, 1912).

LA AGUJA HUECA (LUPIN Y HOLMES) (The Hollow Needle (Lupin versus Holmes)) 1912
A drama in (?) acts by Serrano Viteri and Enrique Griman de Mauro.
Produced in Madrid in 1912.

THE RAFFLE-ING OF SHERLOCK HOLMES 1913
A comedy in one act by N. Thorpe-Mayne.
First produced, as a curtain-raiser to *Improper Peter*, at the Grand Theatre, Fulham, 17 March 1913.

LA TRAGEDIA DE BASKERVILLE (The Baskerville Tragedy) 1915
A drama in five acts by Gonzalo Jover and Enrique Arroyo.
First produced at the Teatro Trueba, Bilbao, 7 Apr 1915.
Sherlock Holmes: Sr Comes. Watson: Sr Socias. Enrique de Baskerville: Sr Del Cerro. Stapleton: Sr Farnos. El Doctor Mortimer: Sr H. del Rio. Barrymore: Sr Sender.
Published by Sociedad de Autores Espagnoles (Madrid, 1915.)

EL VENDEDOR DE CADAVERES O EL TIMO A 'LA GRESHAM' (The Body Seller) 1915
A melodrama in seven acts by M. S. Sucarrato.
Produced in Palma de Mallorca, 1915.
Published by Sociedad de Autores Espagnoles (1915).

HAZANAS DE SHERLOCK HOLMES (Exploits of Sherlock Holmes)
A melodrama in six acts by Emilio Graells Soler and Enrique Casanova.
Performed in Barcelona, c1915.
Sherlock Holmes: Sr Parreno. Mary: Srta Guitart. Laura: Srta Nougues. Lord Enrique: Sr Rodriguez.
Published by Biblioteca Teatro Popular (Barcelona, c1915).

THE CROWN DIAMOND (An Evening with Sherlock Holmes) 1921
A play in one act by Sir Arthur Conan Doyle.

Performed at the London Coliseum, 16 May 1921 for one week, and 30 Aug 1921 for one week.
(Copyright performance at the Hippodrome, Bristol, 2 May 1921.)
Sherlock Holmes: Dennis Neilson-Terry. Dr Watson: R. V. Taylour. Billy: Ronald Hammond. Col Sebastian Moran: Norman Leyland. Sam Merton: Charles Farrell.

THE RETURN OF SHERLOCK HOLMES 1923
A drama in four acts by J. E. Harold Terry and Arthur Rose.
First performed at the Playhouse, Cardiff, 1 Oct 1923 for one week.
First London production at the Princes Theatre, Shaftesbury Avenue, 9 Oct 1923.
Sherlock Holmes: Eille Norwood. Dr Watson: H. G. Stoker. Lady Frances Carfax: Molly Kerr. The Rev Dr Schlessinger: Arthur Cullin. Col Sebastian Moran: Lauderdale Maitland. The Hon Phillip Green: Noel Dainton.
Toured Great Britain throughout 1924. Sherlock Holmes: Eille Norwood.
Produced at the Grand Theatre, Amsterdam, 1 Jan 1924.
Sherlock Holmes: Henry de Vries. Dr Watson: Th. van Schaick.
Produced at the Sonderbros Teater, Copenhagen, 1926 under the title *The Empty House*. Sherlock Holmes: Hermann Florents.
Toured by Burdick and Buckmaster's Company, 1927. Sherlock Holmes: Charles Buckmaster. Dr Watson: Edwin Fraser.
Toured by Tod Slaughter and Company, Oct and Nov 1928. Sherlock Holmes: Tod Slaughter.
Revised version by L. Arthur Rose and Ernest Dudley.
Produced at the New Theatre, Bromley, 20 Jan 1953.
Sherlock Holmes: Geoffrey Edwards. Dr Watson: Jack Lambert. Col Sebastian Moran: Willoughby Goddard.

THE DEVIL'S SERVANT c1927(?)
A mystery drama in five scenes by Steve Knoto.
Apparently devised for performance by a fit-up company, with improvised dialogue and action. Based on the stories *Lady Frances Carfax* and *The Speckled Band*.

THE HOLMESES OF BAKER STREET 1933
A play in three acts by Basil Mitchell.
First performed at the Lyceum Theatre, Edinburgh, 23 Jan 1933 for one week; Princes Theatre, Manchester, 30 Jan for one week; Garrick Theatre, Southport, 6 Feb for one week.
First London production at the Lyric Theatre, 15 Feb 1933, closing on 25 Feb 1933. Then performed at the Streatham Hill Theatre, 6 March 1933 for one week, and the Hippodrome, Golders Green, 13 March 1933 for one week.
Sherlock Holmes: Felix Aylmer. Dr Watson: Sir Nigel Playfair. Shirley

Holmes: Rosemary Ames. Mrs Watson: Eva Moore. Mr Canning: Martin Walker (at Edinburgh, John Loder). Det Insp Withers: Vincent Holman.
Toured British provinces July to December 1933. Sherlock Holmes: Edmund Kennedy.
First American production at the Masque Theatre, New York, 9 Dec 1936 for 54 performances, in an adaptation by William Jourdan Rapp and Leonardo Bercovici.
Sherlock Holmes: Cyril Scott. Dr Watson: Conway Wingfield. Shirley Holmes: Helen Chandler. Mrs Watson: Cecilia Loftus. Mr Canning: Don Dillaway. Inspector Withers: Stuart Casey.

THE GREAT DETECTIVE   1953
A ballet with choreography by Margaret Dale and music by Richard Arnell.
First performed at the Sadler's Wells Theatre, 21 Jan 1953.
The Great Detective: Kenneth Macmillan. His friend the Doctor: Stanley Holden. Innocent Suspect: David Blair. The Infamous Professor: Kenneth Macmillan.
Toured the British provinces in 1953.
The score recorded on Pye LP GGC4048 (GSGC14048 stereo), 1966.

SHERLOCK HOLMES   1953
A melodrama in three acts by Ouida Rathbone.
First produced at the Majestic Theatre, Boston, Massachusetts, 10 Oct 1953 for three weeks.
Produced at the Century Theatre, New York, 30 Oct 1953 for 3 performances.
Sherlock Holmes: Basil Rathbone. Dr Watson: Jack Raine. Mrs Hudson: Elwyn Harvey. Rt Hon Trelawney Hope: John Dodsworth. Arthur Cadogan West: Richard Wendley. Lady Hope: Eileen Peel. Irene Adler: Jarmila Novotna. Lestrade: Bryan Herbert. Professor Moriarty: Thomas Gomez.

THEY MIGHT BE GIANTS   1961
A play by James Goldman.
Presented by Theatre Workshop in association with Robert E. Griffith and Harold S. Prince, at the Theatre Royal, Stratford, London, 28 June 1961. Directed by Joan Littlewood.
Blevins Playfair: Roy Kinnear. Mr Brown: Glynn Edwards. Daisy Playfair: Elizabeth Orion. Justin Playfair: Harry H. Corbett. Dr Mildred Watson: Avis Bunnage. Superintendent Grutt: Roy Godfrey. Mr Small: Royston Tickner. Wilbur Peabody: Brian Murphy.

BAKER STREET   1965
A Musical Adventure of Sherlock Holmes.
Book by Jerome Coopersmith. Music and lyrics by Marian Grudeff and Raymond Jessell.

First performed at the Broadway Theatre, New York City, 16 Feb 1965, closing on 14 Nov 1965 after 313 performances. (Transferred to the Martin Beck Theatre, 3 Nov 1965.)
Sherlock Holmes: Fritz Weaver. Dr Watson: Peter Sallis. Captain Gregg: Patrick Horgan. Mrs Hudson: Paddy Edwards. Inspector Lestrade: Daniel Keyes. Irene Adler: Inga Swenson. Wiggins: Teddy Green. Professor Moriarty: Martin Gabel.
Published by Doubleday and Co Inc (New York, 1966).
The principal musical items were recorded by the cast in New York City on 21 Feb 1965 and issued by MGM on a long-playing record E7000 OC (SE7000C stereo).

SHERLOCK HOLMES AND THE SPECKLED BAND 1968
A drama in two acts by David Buxton.
Performed at the Colchester Repertory Theatre, 3–14 Dec 1968.
Sherlock Holmes: Roger Heathcott. Dr Watson: Clive Rust. Billy: Anthony Martin. Dr Grimesby Rylott: Hal Jeayes. Raschid: Derek Pollitt. Helen Stoner: Pamela Ruddock. Julia Stoner: Angela Ellis. Dr Mortimer: Brian Ellis.

THE HOUND OF THE BASKERVILLES 1971
A drama by Joan Knight.
First produced at the Perth Repertory Theatre, 7 Apr–17 Apr 1971.
Sherlock Holmes: Tim Preece. Dr Watson: Richard Simpson. Dr Mortimer: Andrew Burt. Sir Henry Baskerville: William Corlett. Barrymore: Colin Higgins. Mrs Barrymore: Virginia Stark. Jack Stapleton: Ian Bamforth. Beryl Stapleton: Jean Rimmer.

SHERLOCK'S LAST CASE
A play by Matthew Lang.
First produced at the Open Space Theatre, London, 24 July 1974.
Sherlock Holmes: Julian Glover. Dr Watson: Peter Bayliss. Mrs Hudson: Barbara New. Liza: Kate O'Mara. Mrs Perivale: Lucy Griffiths.

SHERLOCK HOLMES OF BAKER STREET
A play by John Southworth
First produced at Ipswich Drama Centre, 6 Nov 1974.
Sherlock Holmes: Richard Franklin. Dr Watson: Lionel Thomson.
Based on *A Case of Identity*, *The Mazarin Stone* and *The Dying Detective*.

Other Related Stage Pieces

LOCKJAW BONES 1901
A burlesque sketch by J. F. Lambe.
First produced at the Oxford Music Hall, London, 2 Nov 1901.
Lockjaw Bones: George Mozart.
A short travesty of the Gillette Gas Chamber scene.

SHERBERT JONES, or WHO STOLE THE ROLLER SKATES 1911
A burlesque by Hugh Robinson.
First produced at the Kingsway Theatre, London, 20 Sept 1911.

SHYLOCK HYAMS 1915
Thirty minutes of farcical comedy by Arthur Rose.
Performed 21 June 1915, Hammersmith Palace of Varieties, London.
Shylock Hyams: Herbert Landeck.

Sherlock Holmes on Film

All the known films featuring Sherlock Holmes are listed here in chronological order, mostly based on the first date of release, where available.

Many of the synopses in the early film trade magazines were copied verbatim from those supplied by the film companies. Occasionally the names of characters became altered in the process.

SILENT FILMS

SHERLOCK HOLMES BAFFLED
The American Mutoscope & Biograph Co   USA   1900
Filmed April 1900. Cameraman: Arthur Marvin. Length 49ft.
Registered for copyright at the Library of Congress, 24 Feb 1903. A bromide-paper print of this film was deposited at the Library of Congress, and has now been restored to a viewable film.

THE ADVENTURES OF SHERLOCK HOLMES or HELD FOR A RANSOM (GB: SHERLOCK HOLMES or HELD TO RANSOM)
The Vitagraph Co   USA   1903
725ft. Registered at the Library of Congress, 6 Sept 1905. Shown in GB in 1906 and 1907.
Dir: J. Stuart Blackton. Sc: Theodor Liebler.
Sherlock Holmes: Maurice Costello

SHERLOCK HOLMES RETURNS
Production Company (?)   Country (?)   1906–7
250ft.

RIVAL SHERLOCK HOLMES
Ambrosio   Italy   1907

A Pictorial detective story of merit, with many lightning changes of disguise by the detective in his pursuit of the lawbreakers. Exciting scenes and physical encounters are numerous. A sensational subject of superb dramatic effect, without any objectionable features.

Moving Picture World (2 May 1908)

SHERLOCK HOCHMES
Projectograph RT   Hungary   1908
Sherlock Hochmes: Bauman Karoly. The film had a synchronised musical score on gramophone records.

SHERLOCK HOLMES I LIVSFARE (Sherlock Holmes Risks His Life) (GB and USA: SHERLOCK HOLMES)
Nordisk Films Kompagni   Denmark   1908
348m (1141ft). Rel: GB, Oct 1908.
Dir and Sc: Viggo Larsen. Sherlock Holmes: Viggo Larsen. Raffles: Holger Madsen. Billy: Elith Plio.

SHERLOCK HOLMES II (GB: RAFFLES ESCAPES FROM PRISON)
Nordisk   Denmark   1908
210m (689ft). Rel: GB, Nov 1908.
Dir and Sc: Viggo Larsen. Sherlock Holmes: Viggo Larsen. Raffles: Holger Madsen.

SHERLOCK HOLMES III or SHERLOCK HOLMES I GASKJELDEREN (GB: SHERLOCK HOLMES IN THE GAS CELLAR)
(Alternative Danish title: *Det Hemmelige Dokument*; alternative GB title: *The Theft of the State Document*.)
Nordisk   Denmark   1908
275m (902ft). Rel: GB, Dec 1908.
Dir and Sc: Viggo Larsen. Sherlock Holmes: Viggo Larsen.

SHERLOCK HOLMES IN THE GREAT MURDER MYSTERY
Crescent Film Co   USA   1908

> Our picture relates to a crime committed by a Gorilla who escapes from his cage and through circumstancial evidence a young man is accused and is just about to be convicted when through the aid of our hero, Sherlock Holmes, he is freed just in time.
>
> *Moving Picture World* (28 Nov 1908)

SANGERINDENS DIAMANTER (The Singer's Diamonds) (GB: THE THEFT OF THE DIAMONDS)
Nordisk   Denmark   1909
180m (590ft). Rel: Denmark, 20 Jan 1909; GB, 29 Jan 1910. Dir and Sc: Viggo Larsen. Sherlock Holmes: Viggo Larsen.

DROSKE NO 519 (Cab No 519)
Nordisk   Denmark   1909
343m (1125ft). Rel: Denmark, 30 Apr 1909.

Dir and Sc: Viggo Larsen. Sherlock Holmes: Viggo Larsen. Billy: Elith Plio.
Also August Blom.

DEN GRAA DAME (The Grey Lady)
Nordisk   Denmark   1909
307m (1007ft). Rel: Denmark, 27 Aug 1909.
Dir and Sc: Viggo Larsen. Sherlock Holmes: Viggo Larsen. The Uncle:
Gustav Lund. Also Holger Madsen.

THE LATEST TRIUMPH OF SHERLOCK HOLMES (GB title)
Gaumont   France   1909
566ft. Rel: GB, 10 Nov 1909.

SHERLOCK HOLMES
Itala   Italy   1909–10
620ft.

ARSÈNE LUPIN CONTRA SHERLOCK HOLMES
This series comprised five films. The next three listed plus *Die Flucht* (p 138)
and *Arsène Lupins Ende* (p 138).

DER ALTE SEKRETÄR (The Old Secretaire) (GB: ARSÈNE LUPIN)
Vitascope   Germany   1910
345m (1133ft). Rel: Germany, 20 Aug 1910; GB 1 Sept 1910.
Dir: Viggo Larsen. Sherlock Holmes: Viggo Larsen. Arsène Lupin: Paul Otto.

DER BLAUE DIAMANT (The Blue Diamond)
Vitascope GmbH   Germany   1910
430m (1415ft). Rel: Germany, 17 Sept 1910; GB, 29 Oct 1910.
Dir: Viggo Larsen. Sherlock Holmes: Viggo Larsen. Arsène Lupin: Paul Otto.

DIE FALSCHEN REMBRANDTS (The Fake Rembrandts) (GB: THE
TWO REMBRANDTS)
Vitascope GmbH   Germany   1910
295m (968ft). Rel: Germany, 7 Oct 1910; GB, 8 Jan 1911.
Dir: Viggo Larsen. Sherlock Holmes: Viggo Larsen. Arsène Lupin: Paul Otto.

SHERLOCK HOLMES I BONDEFANGERKLØR or DEN STJAALNE
TEGNEBOG (Sherlock Holmes in the Claws of the Confidence Men, or
The Stolen Wallet) (GB: THE CONFIDENCE TRICK)
Nordisk   Denmark   1910
266m (872ft). (?) Rel: GB, 10 Dec 1910.
Sherlock Holmes: Otto Lagoni. Also Axel Boelsen, Ellen Kornbech.

DIE FLUCHT (The Escape)
Vitascope GmbH   Germany   1910
340m. Rel: Germany, 24 Dec 1910.
Dir: Viggo Larsen. Sherlock Holmes: Viggo Larsen. Arsène Lupin: Paul Otto.

FORKLAEDTE BARNEPIGE or DEN FORKLAEDTE
GUVERNANTE (The Bogus Governess)
Nordisk   Denmark   1910
320m (1056ft). Rel: Denmark, 2 Jan 1911; GB, 7 Jan 1911.
Sherlock Holmes: (?).

MEDLEM AF DEN SORTE HAND or MORDET I BAKER STREET
(The Black Hand or Murder in Baker Street)
Nordisk   Denmark   1911
292m (958ft). Rel: Denmark, 2 Jan 1911.
Dir: Holger Rasmussen. Sherlock Holmes: Holger Rasmussen. Also Ingeborg
Rasmussen, Eric Crone, Otto Lagoni. This is probably the film issued by
Nordisk in GB and USA as *The Conspirators* (GB, 10 June 1911; USA, 30 Sept
1911).

MILLIONOBLIGATION (The One Million Bond)
Nordisk   Denmark   1910
310m (1017ft). Rel: Denmark, 14 Jan 1911.
Sherlock Holmes: Alwin Neuss. Also Einar Zangenberg, Alfi Zangenberg.
This is almost certainly the film issued by Nordisk in GB under the title *The
Stolen Legacy* (GB: 21 Jan 1911). It also probably had the alternative title of
Sherlock Holmes's Mesterstykke (Sherlock Holmes's Masterpiece), released in
Germany as *Ein Meisterstück von Sherlock Holmes.*

HOTEL MYSTERIERNE or SHERLOCK HOLMES SIDSTE
BEDRIFT or HOTEL ROTTERNE (The Hotel Mystery or Sherlock
Holmes's Last Exploits or Hotel Rats)
Nordisk   Denmark   1911
255m (836ft). Rel: Denmark, 7 Feb 1911; GB, 8 Feb 1911.
Sherlock Holmes: (?)

ARSÈNE LUPINS ENDE (The End of Arsène Lupin)
Vitascope GmbH   Germany   1911
275m (880ft). Rel: Germany, 4 March 1911; GB, 22 Apr 1911.
Dir: Viggo Larsen. Sherlock Holmes: Viggo Larsen. Arsène Lupin: Paul Otto.

SHERLOCK HOLMES CONTRA PROFESSOR MORYARTY or
DER ERBE VON BLOOMROD (The Heir of Bloomrod)
Vitascope GmbH   Germany   1911

685m Rel: Germany, 29 Apr 1911.
Dir: Viggo Larsen. Sherlock Holmes: Viggo Larsen.

LES AVENTURES DE SHERLOCK HOLMES
Eclair   France   1911
2 reels. Rel: (?)
Dir and Sc: Victorin Jasset. Sherlock Holmes: Henri Gouget. Also Camille
Bardout, Rene d'Auchy, Josette Andriot.

SCHLAU, SCHLAUER, AM SCHLAUESTEN (*Original French title unknown*)
Eclipse   France   1912
462m. Rel: Germany, 12 Oct 1912.
Nat Pinkerton demonstrates his superiority over his jealous rivals, Nick
Winter, Sherlock Holmes and Nick Carter, by tricking them off a train and
keeping the prisoner, the jewels and the glory all for himself. The consequences
of their jealousy have taught them a lesson, 'Seine Kollegen sind vollständig
geschlagen und erkennen Pinkerton von nun ab als ihren Meister an.'

ECLAIR SERIES
This series comprised the eight films following and were all made in GB in
1912. In GB *The Sign of Four* was added to the series. All are adaptations of
Conan Doyle stories. Sherlock Holmes: Georges Treville.

THE SPECKLED BAND
1700ft. Rel: USA, Nov 1912; GB, 27 Oct 1913.

THE REIGATE SQUIRES
1800ft. Rel: USA, Nov 1912; GB, 23 Feb 1914.

THE BERYL CORONET
2300ft. Rel: USA, Nov 1912; GB, 29 Dec 1913.

THE ADVENTURE OF THE COPPER BEECHES
1700ft. Rel: USA, Nov 1912; GB, 25 May 1914.

A MYSTERY OF BOSCOME VALE
1700ft. Rel: USA, Nov 1912; GB, 27 Apr 1914.

THE STOLEN PAPERS
1400ft. Rel: USA, Nov 1912; GB, 30 March 1914.
(From the story *The Naval Treaty*.)

SILVER BLAZE
1300ft. Rel: USA, Nov 1912; GB, 24 Nov 1913.

THE MUSGRAVE RITUAL
1290ft. Rel: USA, Jan 1913; GB, 26 Jan 1914.

SHERLOCK HOLMES SOLVES THE SIGN OF THE FOUR
(GB: THE SIGN OF FOUR)
Thanhouser   USA   1913
2 reels. Rel: USA, 25 Feb 1913; GB, 29 June 1914. Sherlock Holmes: Harry Benham.

USA: GRIFFARD'S CLAW; GB: IN THE GRIP OF THE EAGLE'S
CLAW (*Original Italian title unknown*)
Ambrosio   Italy   1913
2 reels. Rel: USA, 22 Nov 1913; GB, Dec 1913.
> See the famous detective in a flying aeroplane follow the movements of the fleeing kidnapper, and the capture at the villain's moment of triumph.
>   Ambrosio advertisement

SHERLOCK HOLMES CONTRA DR MORS
(?) Vitascope   Germany   (?) 1914
3 reels. Rel: (?) (Shown in Copenhagen, Dec 1914).
Sc: Richard Oswald. Sherlock Holmes: Ferdinand Bonn. Dr Mors: Erich Kähne.

DER HUND VON BASKERVILLE (The Hound of the Baskervilles)
Vitascope GmbH   Germany   1914
1337m. Rel: Germany, June 1914; USA, Jan 1915.
Dir: Rudolph Meinert. Sc: Richard Oswald. Sherlock Holmes: Alwin Neuss. Stapleton: Friedrich Kühne. Barrymore: Andreas von Horn. Miss Lyons: Hanni Weisse. Henry von Baskerville: Erwin Fichtner.

EN RAEDSOM NAT (A Night of Terror) – Germany: EINE
SCHRECKENSNACHT
Filmfabrikken Danmark   Denmark   1914
5 reels. Rel: Denmark, 6 July 1914; Germany, c Jan 1917. With Emilie Sannom.

DAS EINSAME HAUS (The Isolated House) – DER HUND VON
BASKERVILLE II
Union-Vitascope   Germany   1914
1100m. Rel: Germany, 30 Oct 1914; USA, July 1915.
Dir: Rudolf Meinert. Sc: Richard Oswald. Sherlock Holmes: Alwin Neuss. Stapleton: Friedrich Kühne. Barrymore: Andreas von Horn. Miss Lyons: Hanni Weisse. Henry von Baskerville: Erwin Fichtner.

HVEM ER HUN? (Where is She?) – Germany: WER IST SIE?
Filmfabrikken Danmark   Denmark   1914
1827m. Rel: Denmark, 7 Dec 1914; Germany, Nov-Dec 1916.
Dir and Sc: Em Gregers. Actors: Em Gregers, Nathalie Krause, Jon Iversen.

A STUDY IN SCARLET
The Samuelson Film Mfg Co Ltd   GB   1914
5749ft. Rel: GB, 28 Dec 1914.
Dir: George Pearson. Sc: Harry Engholm. Sherlock Holmes: James Braging-ton. Jefferson Hope: Fred Paul. Lucy Ferrier: Agnes Glynne. Lucy Ferrier as a child: Winifred Pearson. John Ferrier: James Le Fre. Brigham Young: Harry Paulo.

A STUDY IN SCARLET
Gold Seal (Universal)   USA   1914
2 reels. Rel: USA, 29 Dec 1914.
Dir: Francis Ford. Sc: Grace Cunard. Sherlock Holmes: Francis Ford.

DAS UNHEIMLICHE ZIMMER (The Uncanny Room) – DER HUND VON BASKERVILLE III
Greenbaum-Film GmbH   Germany   1915
3 reels. Rel: Germany, Apr 1915.
Dir and Sc: Richard Oswald. Sets: Herman Warm. Sherlock Holmes: Alwin Neuss. Also Friedrich Kühne, Erwin Fichtner, Andreas von Horn and Tatjana Irrah.

WIE ENTSTAND DER HUND VON BASKERVILLE (How the Hound of the Baskervilles Arose) – DER HUND VON BASKERVILLE IV – also known as DIE SAGE VOM HUND VON BASKERVILLE
Greenbaum-Film GmbH   Germany   1915
809m. Rel: (?)
Dir and Sc: Richard Oswald. Sherlock Holmes: Alwin Neuss. Also Friedrich Kühne, Erwin Fichtner, Hilde Bork, Andreas von Horn.

DAS DUNKLE SCHLOSS (The Dark Castle) – DER HUND VON BASKERVILLE III
Projections AG Union   Germany   1915
3 reels. Rel: Germany, Aug 1915.
Dir: Willy Zehn. Sherlock Holmes: Eugen Burg. Also Friedrich Zellnik, Hanni Weisse, Friedrich Kühne.

EIN SCHREI IN DER NACHT (A Scream in the Night)
Decla   Germany   1915
3 reels. Rel: Germany, Dec 1915.
Dir: Alwin Neuss. Sc: Paul Rosenhayn. Sherlock Holmes: Alwin Neuss. Also Eddie Seefeld, Aenne Köhler, Reinhold Pasch, Adolf Suchanek.

WILLIAM VOSS
Meinert-Film   Germany   1915
1000m. Rel: Germany, Dec 1915.
Dir and Sc: Rudolph Meinert. Sherlock Holmes: (?) William Voss: Theodor Burgardt.

SHERLOCK HOLMES
Essanay   USA   1916
7 reels. Rel: USA, 15 May 1916; GB, Oct 1917.
Dir: William Gillette and Arthur Berthelet. Sherlock Holmes: William Gillette. Dr Watson: Edward Fielding. Professor Moriarty: Ernest Maupin.

THE VALLEY OF FEAR
The Samuelson Film Mfg Co Ltd   GB   1916
6500ft. Rel: GB, May 1916; USA, Jan 1917.
Dir: Alexander Butler. Sc: Harry Engholm. Sherlock Holmes: H. A. Saintsbury. Dr Watson: Arthur M. Cullin. Professor Moriarty: Booth Conway.

SHERLOCK HOLMES AUF URLAUB (Sherlock Holmes on Leave)
(?)   Germany   1916
3 reels. Rel: (?)
Dir and Sc: Karl Schonfeld.

SHERLOCK HOLMES NÄCHTLICHE BEGEGNUNG
(Sherlock Holmes's Nocturnal Encounter)
(?)   Germany   1917
4 reels.

DER ERDSTROMMOTOR (The Earthquake Motor)
Kowo-Film AG   Germany   1917
1459m. Rel: Germany, 12 Aug 1921.
Dir: Karl Heinz Wolff. Sc: Paul Rosenhayn. Sherlock Holmes: Hugo Flink.

DIE KASETTE (The Casket)
Kowo-Film AG   Germany   1917
1214m. Rel: Germany, 12 Oct 1921.
Dir: Karl Heinz Wolff. Sc: Paul Rosenhayn. Sherlock Holmes: Hugo Flink. First advertised as *Der Geheimnisvolle Hut*, then announced as *Das Ratsel der Ballnacht*, this film was eventually released as *Die Kasette*.

DER SCHLANGENRING (The Snake Ring)
Kowo-Film AG   Germany   1917
4 reels. Rel: (?)
Dir: Karl Heinz Wolff. Sc: Paul Rosenhayn. Sherlock Holmes: Hugo Flink.

DIE INDISCHE SPINNE (The Indian Spider)
Kowo-Film AG   Germany   1918
Dir: Karl Heinz Wolff. Sc: Paul Rosenhayn. Sherlock Holmes: Hugo Flink.
Reported as in production. Possibly not completed.

ROTTERDAM – AMSTERDAM
Messter-Film   Germany   1918
1145m. Rel: Germany, Feb 1918.
Dir: Viggo Larsen. Sc: Richard Hutter. Sherlock Holmes: Viggo Larsen.

WAS ER IM SPIEGEL SAH (What He Saw in the Mirror)
Kowo GmbH   Germany   1918
4 reels. Rel: (?)
Dir: Karl Heinz Wolff. Sherlock Holmes: Ferdinand Bonn.

DIE GIFTPLOMBE (The Poisoned Seal)
Kowo GmbH   Germany   1918
4 reels. Rel: (?)
Dir: Karl Heinz Wolff. Sherlock Holmes: Ferdinand Bonn.

DAS SCHICKSAL DER RENATE YONGK (The Fate of Renate
Yongk)
Kowo GmbH   Germany   1918
1315m. Rel: Germany, 7 Jan 1922.
Dir: Karl Heinz Wolff. Sc: Werner Bernhardy. Sherlock Holmes: Ferdinand
Bonn.

DIE DOSE DES KARDINALS (The Cardinal's Snuffbox)
Kowo GmbH   Germany   1918
Length: (?) Rel: (?)
Dir: Karl Heinz Wolff. Sc: Otto Schubert-Stevens. Sherlock Holmes: Ferdin-
and Bonn.

DREI TAGE TOT (Three Days Dead)
Bioscop Konzern   Germany (?)   1919
Length: (?) Rel: Germany, 5 March 1919.
Dir: Nils Chrysander.

DER MORD IM SPLENDID HOTEL (Murder in the Hotel Splendid)
Kowo GmbH   Germany   1919
Length: (?) Rel: (?)
Dir: Karl Heinz Wolff. Sherlock Holmes: Kurt Brenkendorff.

DR MACDONALDS SANATORIUM (DER HUND VON BASKER-VILLE V)

Greenbaum-Film GmbH   Germany   1920
1514m. Rel: (?)
Dir: Willy Zehn. Sc: Robert Liebmann. Sherlock Holmes: Erich Kaiser-Titz (?)

DAS HAUS OHNE FENSTER (The House without Windows) – DER HUND VON BASKERVILLE VI

Greenbaum-Film Gmbh   Germany   1920
1732m. Rel: (?)
Dir: Willy Zehn. Sc: Robert Liebmann. Actors: Lu Jürgens, Erwin Fichtner, Ludwig Rex.

ADVENTURES OF SHERLOCK HOLMES

First series by Stoll Picture Productions Ltd made in GB in 1921.
Dir: Maurice Elvey. Sc: William J. Elliott. Cam: W. Germain Burger.
Sherlock Holmes: Eille Norwood. Dr Watson: Hubert Willis.

THE DYING DETECTIVE

2273ft. Rel: GB, May 1921.
Culverton Smith: Cecil Humphreys. Mrs Hudson: Madame d'Esterre. Staples: J. R. Tozer.

THE DEVIL'S FOOT

2514ft. Rel: GB, May 1921.
Mortimer Tregennis: Harvey Brabham. Dr Leon Sterndale: Hugh Buckler.

A CASE OF IDENTITY

2610ft. Rel: GB, May 1921.
Mary Sutherland: Edna Flugrath. James Windibank: Nelson Ramsey. Mrs Windibank: Nessie Blackford.

THE YELLOW FACE

2020ft. Rel: GB, May 1921.
Jack Grant Munro: Clifford Heatherley. Effie Grant Munro: Norma Whalley. The negress: L. Allen. The child: Master Robey.

THE RED-HEADED LEAGUE

2140ft. Rel: GB, June 1921.
Jabez Wilson: Teddy Arundel. Vincent Spaulding: H. Townsend. Inspector Lestrade: Arthur Bell.

THE RESIDENT PATIENT

2404ft. Rel: GB, June 1921.
Dr Percy Trevelyan: C. Pitt Chatham. Mr Blessington: Judd Green. Moffatt:

Wallace Bosco. Inspector Lestrade: Arthur Bell. Maid: Beatrice Templeton. Mrs Hudson: Madame d'Esterre.

A SCANDAL IN BOHEMIA
2100ft. Rel: GB, June 1921.
The King of Bohemia: Alfred Drayton. Irene Adler: Joan Beverley. Mrs Hudson: Madame d'Esterre. Godfrey Norton: Miles Mander. Maid: Annie Esmond.

THE MAN WITH THE TWISTED LIP
2412ft. Rel: GB, June 1921.
Mrs Hudson: Madame d'Esterre. Neville St Clair: Robert Vallis. Mrs St Clair: Paulette del Baye.

THE BERYL CORONET
2340ft. Rel: GB, July 1921.
Sc: Charles Barnett. Alexander Holder: Henry Vibart. Mary: Mollie Adair. Arthur Holder: Laurence Anderson. Sir George Burnwell: Jack Selfridge. Mrs Hudson: Madame d'Esterre.

THE NOBLE BACHELOR
2100ft. Rel: GB, July 1921.
Hatty Doran: Temple Bell. Francis Hay Moulton: Frederick Earle. Mrs Hudson: Madame d'Esterre. Lord Robert St Simon: Cyril Percival. Aloysius Doran: Mr Arlton. Flora Millar: Miss Middleton.

THE COPPER BEECHES
2193ft. Rel: GB, July 1921.
Violet Hunter: Madge White. Jephro Rucastle: Lyell Johnston. Mrs Rucastle: Lottie Blackford. Toller: Fred Raynham. Mrs Toller: Eve McCarthy. Japhet: William J. Elliott Jnr. Roger Wilson: Bobbie Harwood. Ada Repson: Madge White. Miss Stoper: C. Nicholls. Inspector Lestrade: Arthur Bell.

THE EMPTY HOUSE
1800ft. Rel: GB, July 1921.
Col Sebastian Moran: Sidney Seaward. Hon Ronald Adair: Austin Fairman. Mrs Adair: J. Gelardi. Sir Charles Ridge: Cecil Kerr. Inspector Lestrade: Arthur Bell.

THE TIGER OF SAN PEDRO
2080ft. Rel: GB, July 1921.
Mrs Hudson: Madame d'Esterre. Inspector Lestrade: Arthur Bell. John Scott Eccles: George Harrington. Mr Henderson: Lewis Gilbert. Aloysius Garcia: Arthur Walcott. Miss Burnett: Valia Veritskeya.
From the story *Wisteria Lodge*.

THE PRIORY SCHOOL
2100ft. Rel: GB, Aug 1921.

Sc: Charles Barnett. Mrs Hudson: Madame d'Esterre. Dr Thorneycroft Huxtable: Leslie English. Duke of Holdernesse: C. H. Croker-King. Duchess of Holdernesse: Irene Rooke. Lord Saltire: Patrick Kay. James Wilder: Cecil Kerr. Reuben Hayes: Tom Ronald. De Castelet: Allen Leamy.

THE SOLITARY CYCLIST
2140ft. Rel: GB, Aug 1921.
Violet Relph: Violet Hewitt. Bob Carruthers: R. D. Silvester. Jack Woodley: Alan Jeayes. Mrs Hudson: Madame d'Esterre.

THE HOUND OF THE BASKERVILLES
5500ft. Rel: GB, 8 Aug 1921.
Dr Mortimer: Alan Jeayes. Sir Henry Baskerville: Rex McDougall. John Stapleton: Lewis Gilbert. Beryl Stapleton: Betty Campbell. Barrymore: Fred Raynham. Mrs Hudson: Madame d'Esterre. Sir Charles Baskerville: Robert English. Selden: Robert Vallis. Mrs Barrymore: Miss Walker.

FURTHER ADVENTURES OF SHERLOCK HOLMES

Second Stoll series made in GB in 1922 (the next fifteen listed).
Dir: George Ridgewell. Sc: Patrick L. Mannock, Geoffrey H. Malins. Cam: Alfred H. Moses. Art Dir: Walter W. Murton. Sherlock Holmes: Eille Norwood. Dr Watson: Hubert Willis.

CHARLES AUGUSTUS MILVERTON
1900ft. Rel: GB, March 1922.
Charles Augustus Milverton: George Foley. Det Insp Stanley Hopkins: Teddy Arundel. Mrs Hudson: Madame d'Esterre. The Countess of Eastleigh: Tony Edgar-Bruce. Agatha: Edith Bishop. Cook: Annie Hughes. Butler: Harry J. Worth.

THE ABBEY GRANGE
2193ft. Rel: GB, March 1922.
Det Insp Stanley Hopkins: Teddy Arundel. Mrs Hudson: Madame d'Esterre. Lady Brackenstall: Madeleine Seymour. Sir Eustace Brackenstall: Lawford Davidson. Captain Jack Croker: Leslie Stiles. Theresa Wright: Madge Tree.

THE NORWOOD BUILDER
2067ft. Rel: GB, March 1922.
Det Insp Stanley Hopkins: Teddy Arundel. Mrs Hudson: Madame d'Esterre. Jonas Oldacre: Fred Wright. John Hector MacFarlane: Cyril Raymond. Mrs MacFarlane: Laura Walker.

THE REIGATE SQUIRES
1885ft. Rel: GB, March 1922.
Colonel Hayter: Arthur Lumley. Det Insp Stanley Hopkins: Teddy Arundel. Squire Cunningham: Teddy O'Neil. Alec Cunningham: Richard Atwood. William Kirwan: C. Seguin. Mrs Hudson: Madame d'Esterre.

THE NAVAL TREATY
1536ft. Rel: GB, Apr 1922.
Percy Phelps: Jack Hobbs. Joseph Harrison: Frances Duguid. Annie Harrison: Nancy May.

THE SECOND STAIN
2179ft. Rel: GB, Apr 1922.
Det Insp Stanley Hopkins: Teddy Arundel. Mrs Hudson: Madame d'Esterre. Trelawney Hope: A. Scott-Gatty. Lady Hilda Trelawney Hope: Dorothy Fane. Eduardo Lucas: W. Bosco. Mme Henri Fournaye: Maria Minetti. Lord Bellinger: Cecil Ward.

THE RED CIRCLE
1770ft. Rel: GB, Apr 1922.
Det Insp Stanley Hopkins: Teddy Arundel. Mrs Hudson: Madame d'Esterre. Emilia Lucca: Sybil Archdale. Giuseppe Gorgiano: Maresco Marescini. Gennaro Lucca: Bertram Burleigh. Mr Leverton: Tom Beaumont. Mrs Warren: Esme Hubbard.

THE SIX NAPOLEONS
1753ft. Rel: GB, Apr 1922.
Det Insp Stanley Hopkins: Teddy Arundel. Mrs Hudson: Madame d'Esterre. Beppo: George Bellamy. Pietro Venucci: Jack Raymond. Lucretia Venucci: Alice Moffatt.

BLACK PETER
1776ft. Rel: GB, May 1922.
Det Insp Stanley Hopkins: Teddy Arundel. Captain Peter Carey: Fred Paul. Patrick Cairns: Hugh Buckler. John Hopley Neligan: Jack Jarman. Mr Neligan Snr: Fred Rains. Mrs Carey: Mrs Hubert Willis. Miss Carey: Miss Willis.

THE BRUCE-PARTINGTON PLANS
2130ft. Rel: GB, May 1922.
Det Insp Stanley Hopkins: Teddy Arundel. Colonel Valentine Walter: Ronald Power. Hugo Oberstein: Edward Sorley. Arthur Cadogan West: Malcolm Tod. Mycroft Holmes: Lewis Gilbert. Sidney Johnson: Leslie Brittain.

THE STOCKBROKER'S CLERK
1841ft. Rel: GB, May 1922.
Hall Pycroft: Olaf Hytten. Arthur Pinner: Aubrey Fitzgerald. Beddington: George Ridgewell.

THE BOSCOMBE VALLEY MYSTERY
2410ft. Rel: GB, May 1922.
Det Insp Stanley Hopkins: Teddy Arundel. Charles McCarthy: Ray Raymond. James McCarthy: Hal Martin. John Turner: Fred Raynham. Alice Turner: Thelma Murray.

THE MUSGRAVE RITUAL
1698ft. Rel: GB, June 1922.
Reginald Musgrave: Geoffrey Wilmer. Richard Brunton: Clifton Boyne. Rachel Howells: Betty Chester.

THE GOLDEN PINCE-NEZ
1630ft. Rel: GB, June 1922.
Det Insp Stanley Hopkins: Teddy Arundel. Professor Sergius Coram: Cecil Morton York. Mrs Anna Coram: Norma Whalley.

THE GREEK INTERPRETER
1796ft. Rel: GB, June 1922.
Det Insp Stanley Hopkins: H. Wheeler. Mrs Hudson: Madame d'Esterre. Mr Melas: Cecil Dane. Harold Latimer: J. R. Tozer. Wilson Kemp: Robert Vallis. Sophy Kratides: Edith Saville. Paul Kratides: L. Andre.

SHERLOCK HOLMES (GB: MORIARTY)
Goldwyn Pictures   USA   1922
8200ft. Rel: USA, 29 Oct 1922; GB, 29 Jan 1923.
Dir: Albert Parker. Prod: F. J. Godsol. Cam: J. Roy Hunt. Sherlock Holmes: John Barrymore. Dr Watson: Roland Young. Professor Moriarty: Gustav von Seyffertitz. Alice Faulkner: Carol Dempster. Madge Larrabee: Hedda Hopper. Forman Wells: William H. Powell. Craigin: Louis Wolheim.

THE LAST ADVENTURES OF SHERLOCK HOLMES

The third and final Stoll series made in GB in 1923 (the next fifteen listed).
Dir: George Ridgewell. Sc: Geoffrey H. Malins, P. L. Mannock. Cam: Alfred H. Moses. Art Dir: Walter W. Murton. Film Ed: Challis N. Sanderson. Sherlock Holmes: Eille Norwood. Dr Watson: Hubert Willis.

SILVER BLAZE
2077ft. Rel: GB, March 1923.
Silas Brown: Sam Austin. Colonel Ross: Knighton Small. Straker: Sam Marsh. Mrs Straker: Norma Whalley. Groom: Bert Barclay. Insp Gregory: Tom Beaumont.

THE SPECKLED BAND
1803ft. Rel: GB, 19 March 1923.
Mrs Hudson: Madame d'Esterre. Dr Grimesby Rylott: Lewis Gilbert. Helen Stonor: Cynthia Murtagh. Julia Stonor: Jane Graham. Baboon: H. Wilson. Also Celia Bird.

THE GLORIA SCOTT
2070ft. Rel: GB, 19 March 1923.
James Trevor: Fred Raynham. Victor Trevor: Reginald Fox. Hudson: Laurie

Leslie. Jack Prendergast: Ray Raymond. Evans: Ernest Shannon. Also Charles Barratt.

THE BLUE CARBUNCLE
1866ft. Rel: GB, Apr 1923.
Mrs Hudson: Madame d'Esterre. Peterson: Douglas Payne. Henry Baker: Sebastian Smith. James Ryder: Gordon Hopkirk. Catherine Cusack: Miss Hanbury. Breckinridge: Archie Hunter. Mrs Oakshott: Mary Mackintosh.

THE ENGINEER'S THUMB
2026ft. Rel: GB, Apr 1923.
Inspector Gregory: Tom Beaumont. Heatherly: Bertram Burleigh. Colonel Lysander Stark: Henry Latimer. The Girl: Mercy Hatton. Ferguson: Ward McAllister.

HIS LAST BOW
1539ft. Rel: GB, Apr 1923.
Von Bork: Nelson Ramsay. Baron von Herling: R. van Courtland. Martha: Kate Gurney. The Premier: Alec Flood. The Foreign Minister: Ralph Forster. Inspector Gregory: Tom Beaumont. Officer: Watts Phillips.

THE CARDBOARD BOX
1801ft. Rel: GB, May 1923.
Inspector Gregory: Tom Beaumont. James Browner: John Butt. Mary Browner: Hilda Anthony. Alec Fairbairn: Eric Lugg. Miss Cushing: Maud Wulff.

THE DISAPPEARANCE OF LADY FRANCES CARFAX
1818ft. Rel: GB, May 1923.
Hon Phillip Green: David Hawthorne. Lady Frances Carfax: Evelyn Cecil. Holy Peters: Cecil Morton York. Mrs Peters: Madge Tree. Marie Devine: Dorothy Wilkins. Inspector Gregory: Tom Beaumont.

THE THREE STUDENTS
2448ft. Rel: GB, May 1923.
Soames: William Lugg. Bannister: A. Harding Steerman. Gilchrist: L. Verne.

THE MISSING THREE-QUARTER
2200ft. Rel: GB, June 1923.
Mrs Hudson: Madame d'Esterre. Cyril Overton: Hal Martin. Lord Mount-James: Cliff Davies. Dr Leslie Armstrong: Albert E. Rayner. Godfrey Staunton: Leigh Gabell. Hotel Porter: Jack Raymond.

THE MYSTERY OF THOR BRIDGE
2071ft. Rel: GB, June 1923.
Mrs Hudson: Madame d'Esterre. Mr Gibson: A. B. Imeson. Miss Dunbar: Violet Graham. Mrs Gibson: Noel Grahame. Inspector: Harry J. Worth.

THE STONE OF MAZARIN
1873ft. Rel: GB, June 1923.
Insp Gregory: Tom Beaumont. Count Sylvius: Lionel d'Aragon. Merton: Laurie Leslie.

THE DANCING MEN
2387ft. Rel: GB, July 1923.
Hilton Cubitt: Frank Goldsmith. Slaney: Wally Bosco. Mrs Cubitt: Dezma du May.

THE CROOKED MAN
2228ft. Rel: GB, July 1923.
Henry Wood: Jack Hobbs. Mrs Barclay: Gladys Jennings. Miss Morrison: Dora de Winton. Major Murphy: Richard Lindsay.

THE FINAL PROBLEM
1686ft. Rel: GB, July 1923.
Professor Moriarty: Percy Standing. Inspector Gregory: Tom Beaumont. Scout: P. Francis.

THE SIGN OF FOUR
Stoll Picture Productions Ltd   GB   1923
6750ft. Rel: GB, 3 Sept 1923.
Dir and Sc: Maurice Elvey. Cam: John J. Cox. Art Dir: Walter W. Murton. Sherlock Holmes: Eille Norwood. Dr Watson: Arthur Cullin. Mary Morston: Isobel Elsom. Abdullah Khan: Fred Raynham. Jonathan Small: Norma Page. Thaddeus Sholto: Humberston Wright. Inspector Athelney Jones: Arthur Bell. Mrs Hudson: Madame d'Esterre. Tonga: Henry Wilson.

> It was considered that Hubert Willis, who had played Dr Watson in the previous 46 films, was too old for Watson in this story, since Watson has to woo and marry Mary Morstan. So they chose for the role Arthur Cullin, who looked like a middle-aged provincial butler.
>
> Eille Norwood

DER HUND VON BASKERVILLE
Erda-Film-Produktions GmbH   Germany   1929
2382m. Rel: Germany, 28 Aug 1929.
Dir: Richard Oswald. Sc: Herbert Juttke and G. C. Klaren.
Sherlock Holmes: Carlyle Blackwell. Dr Watson: Georges Seroff.

SOUND FILMS

THE RETURN OF SHERLOCK HOLMES
Paramount   USA   1929
7102ft. Rel: USA, 25 Oct 1929; GB, 4 Aug 1930.
Dir: Basil Dean and Clive Brook. Sc: Basil Dean and Garret Fort. Sherlock

Holmes: Clive Brook. Dr Watson: H. Reeves Smith. Professor Moriarty: Harry T. Morey. Colonel Sebastian Moran: Donald Crisp. Roger Longmore: Hubert Druce. Mary Watson: Betty Lawford.

MURDER WILL OUT (A Travesty of Detective Mysteries)
Paramount USA 1930
A sketch in the film revue *Paramount on Parade*.
Length: (?) Rel: USA, 19 Apr 1930; GB, 16 March 1931.
Dir: (?) Sherlock Holmes: Clive Brook. Philo Vance: William Powell. Sergeant Heath: Eugene Pallette. Dr Fu Manchu: Warner Oland. Victim: Jack Oakie.

THE SLEEPING CARDINAL (USA: SHERLOCK HOLMES'S FATAL HOUR)
Twickenham Film Studios Ltd GB 1931
7648ft. 84min. Rel: GB, 20 July 1931; USA, July 1931.
Dir: Leslie Hiscott. Sc: Leslie Hiscott and Cyril Twyford. Sherlock Holmes: Arthur Wontner. Dr Watson: Ian Fleming. Mrs Hudson: Minnie Rayner. Ronald Adair: Leslie Perrins. Kathleen Adair: Jane Welsh. Colonel Henslowe: Norman McKinnel. Colonel Sebastian Moran: Louis Goodrich. Inspector Lestrade: Phillip Hewland.
Based on *The Empty House* and *The Final Problem*.

THE SPECKLED BAND
British & Dominion GB 1931
90min. Rel: GB, 3 Nov 1931.
Dir: Jack Raymond. Sc: W. P. Lipscomb. Sherlock Holmes: Raymond Massey. Dr Watson: Athole Stewart. Dr Rylott: Lyn Harding.

THE HOUND OF THE BASKERVILLES
Gainsborough Pictures GB 1932
6761ft. 75min. Rel: GB, 22 Feb 1932.
Dir and Sc: Gareth Gundrey. Additional dialogue by Edgar Wallace. Prod: Michael Balcon. Sherlock Holmes: Robert Rendel. Dr Watson: Fred Lloyd. Sir Henry Baskerville: John Stuart. Stapleton: Reginald Bach. Beryl Stapleton: Heather Angel. Dr Mortimer: Wilfred Shine. Sir Hugo Baskerville: Sam Livesey. Barrymore: Henry Hallatt. Mrs Laura Lyons: Elizabeth Vaughan. Mrs Barrymore: Sybil Jane.

THE MISSING REMBRANDT
Twickenham Film Studios Ltd GB 1932
7588ft. 84min. Rel: GB, Aug 1932.
Dir: Leslie Hiscott. Sc: H. Fowler Mear and Cyril Twyford. Sherlock Holmes: Arthur Wontner. Dr Watson: Ian Fleming. Mrs Hudson: Minnie Rayner.

Baron von Guntermann: Francis L. Sullivan. Carlo Ravelli: Dini Galvani.
Claud Holford: Miles Mander. Lady Violet Lumsden: Jane Welsh. Marquis
de Chaminade: Anthony Holles. Manning: Herbert Lomas. Pinkerton Agent:
Ben Welden. Chang Wu: Takase. Insp Lestrade: Philip Hewland.
Partly based on *Charles Augustus Milverton*.

THE SIGN OF FOUR
Associated Radio Pictures   GB   1932
6897ft. 76min. Rel: GB, Sept 1932.
Dir: Graham Cutts. Sc: W. P. Lipscomb. Sherlock Holmes: Arthur Wontner.
Dr Watson: Ian Hunter. Mrs Hudson: Claire Greet. Mary Morston: Isla
Bevan. Athelney Jones: Gilbert Davis. Jonathan Small: Ben Soutten. Captain
Morstan: Edgar Norfolk. Major Sholto: Herbert Lomas. Thaddeus Sholto:
Miles Malleson. Bailey: Roy Emerton. Bartholomew Sholto: Kynaston Reeves.
Tonga: Togo.

SHERLOCK HOLMES
Fox   USA   1932
65min. Rel: USA, 11 Nov 1932; GB, Jan 1933.
Dir: William K. Howard. Sc: Bayard Veiller. Sherlock Holmes: Clive Brook.
Dr Watson: Reginald Owen. Alice Faulkner: Miriam Jordan. Professor
Moriarty: Ernest Torrence. Billy: Howard Leeds. Colonel Gore-King: Alan
Mowbray. Judge: Montague Shaw. Chaplain: Arnold Lucy. Hans Dreiaugen:
Lucien Prival. Manuel Lopez: Roy D'Arcy. Homer-Jones: Stanley Fields.
Al: Eddie Dillon. Gaston Roux: Robert Graves Jnr.

LELICEK VE SLUZBACH SHERLOCKA HOLMESE (Lelicek
in the Service of Sherlock Holmes)
Elektafilm AS   Czechoslovakia   1932
2044m. Rel: (?)
Dir: Karel Lamac. Sc: Vaclav Wasserman. Prod: Jan Reiter. Adaptation: Hugo
Vavrise. Cam: Otto Heller, Jan Stallich. Sherlock Holmes: Martin Fric.
Frantisek Lelicek and Fernando XXIII, King of Portorico: Vlasta Burian.
Jeho Sluha James (footman): Fred Bulin. Queen Kralovna: Lida Baarova.
Conchita: Eva Jansenova. Prime Minister: Theodor Pistek. Court Marshal:
Cenek Slegl. Royal Officer: Zvonimir Regez. Photographer: Eman Fiala.

A STUDY IN SCARLET
World Wide   USA   1933
6972ft. 75min. Rel: USA, Apr 1933; GB, Jan 1934.
Dir: Edwin L. Marin. Sc: Robert Florey. Cont and Dial: Reginald Owen.
Sherlock Holmes: Reginald Owen. Dr Watson: Warburton Gamble. Mrs
Hudson: Tempe Pigott. Mrs Pyke: Anna May Wong. Eileen Forrester: June
Clyde. Merrydew: Alan Dinehart. John Stanford: John Warburton. Inspector

Lestrade: Alan Mowbray. Jabez Wilson: J. M. Kerrigan. Mrs Murphy: Doris Lloyd. Dolly: Leila Bennett. Baker: Cecil Reynolds. Captain Pyke: Wyndham Standing. Dearing: Halliwell Hobbes. Ay Yet: Tetsu Komai.

THE TRIUMPH OF SHERLOCK HOLMES
Real Art Productions Ltd   GB   1935
7544ft. 84min. Rel: GB, 26 Aug 1935.
Dir: Leslie Hiscott. Sc: H. Fowler Mear and Cyril Twyford. Prod: Julius Hagen. Sherlock Holmes: Arthur Wontner. Dr Watson: Ian Fleming. Professor Moriarty: Lyn Harding. Mrs Hudson: Minnie Rayner. John Douglas: Leslie Perrins. Ettie Douglas: Jane Carr. Inspector Lestrade: Charles Mortimer. Cecil Barker: Michael Shepley. Ted Balding: Ben Weldon. Boss McGinty: Roy Emerton. Ames: Conway Dixon. Colonel Sebastian Moran: Wilfred Caithness. Jacob Shafter: Ernest Lynds. Captain Marvin: Edmund D'Alby. Based on *The Valley of Fear.*

DER HUND VON BASKERVILLE
Ondra-Lamac-Film GmbH   Germany   1937
2255m (7398ft). Rel: Germany, 12 Jan 1937.
Dir: Karl Lamac. Sc: Carla von Stackelberg. Sherlock Holmes: Bruno Güttner. Dr Watson: Fritz Odemar. Lord Henry Baskerville: Peter Voss. Lord Charles Baskerville: Friedrich Kayssler. Barrymore: Fritz Rasp. Frau Barrymore: Lilly Schönborn. Stapleton: Erich Ponto. Dr Mortimer: Ernest Rotmund. Beryl Vendeleure: Alice Brandt. Holmes's Landlady: Gertrud Walle. Convict: Paul Rehkopf. In prologue: Lady Baskerville, Hanna Waag; Lord Hugo Baskerville, Arthur Malkowski.

SHERLOCK HOLMES: DIE GRAUE DAME (The Grey Lady)
Neue Film KG   Germany 1937
2517m (8258ft). Rel: Germany, 26 Feb 1937.
Dir: Erich Engels. Sc: Erich Engels and Hans Heuer. Jimmy Ward (Sherlock Holmes): Hermann Speelmans. Maria Iretzkaja: Trude Marlen. Lola: Elisabeth Wendt. Baranoff: Edwin Jürgensen. Harry Morrel: Theo Shall. Inspector Brown: Ernst Karchow. John, Ward's servant: Werner Finck. Jack Clark: Werner Scharf. James Hewitt: Hans Halden. Archibald Pepperkorn: Henry Lorenzen. Wilson: Reinhold Bernt. Frau Miller: Eva Tinschmann.

SILVER BLAZE (USA: MURDER AT THE BASKERVILLES)
Twickenham Film Productions Ltd   GB   1937
6258ft. Rel: GB, 15 July 1937.
Dir: Thomas Bentley. Sc: H. Fowler Mear, Arthur Macrae. Sherlock Holmes: Arthur Wontner. Dr Watson: Ian Fleming. Professor Moriarty: Lyn Harding. Inspector Lestrade: John Turnbull. Colonel Ross: Robert Horton. Sir Henry Baskerville: Lawrence Grossmith. Diana Baskerville: Judy Gunn. Jack Trevor:

Arthur Macrae. Colonel Moran: Arthur Coullett. John Straker: Martin Walker. Mrs Straker: Eve Gray. Miles Stamford: Gilbert Davies. Mrs Hudson: Minnie Rayner. Silas Brown: D. J. Williams. Bert Prince: Ralph Truman. Stableboy: Ronald Shiner.

DER MANN, DER SHERLOCK HOLMES WAR (The Man who Was Sherlock Holmes)
UFA   Germany   1937
3072m (10,079ft). Rel: Germany, 15 July 1937.
Dir: Karl Hartl. Sc: R. A. Stemmle and Karl Hartl. Sherlock Holmes: Hans Albers. Dr Watson: Heinz Rühmann. Mary Berry: Marieluise Claudius. Jane Berry: Hansi Knotek. Madama Ganymar: Hilde Weissner. Monsieur Lapin: Siegfried Schurenberg. The man who laughed (Sir Conan Doyle): Paul Bildt. Polizei-Director: Franz W. Schröder-Schrom.
Shown on West German television 31 Jan 1964.

THE HOUND OF THE BASKERVILLES
Twentieth Century-Fox   USA   1939
7169ft. Rel: USA, Apr 1939; GB, Sept 1939.
Dir: Sidney Lanfield. Sc: Ernest Pascal. Sherlock Holmes: Basil Rathbone. Dr Watson: Nigel Bruce. Sir Henry Baskerville: Richard Greene. Beryl Stapleton: Wendy Barrie. Dr James Mortimer: Lionel Atwill. Barryman: John Carradine. Frankland: Barlow Borland. Mrs Jennifer Mortimer: Beryl Mercer. John Stapleton: Morton Lowry. Sir Hugo Baskerville: Ralph Forbes. Cabby: E. E. Clive. Mrs Barryman: Eily Malyon. Convict: Henry Cording. Mrs Hudson: Mary Gordon.

THE ADVENTURES OF SHERLOCK HOLMES (GB: SHERLOCK HOLMES)
Twentieth Century-Fox   USA   1939
81min. Rel: USA, Aug 1939; GB, March 1940.
Dir: Alfred Werker. Sc: Edwin Blum and William Drake. Sherlock Holmes: Basil Rathbone. Dr Watson: Nigel Bruce. Ann Brandon: Ida Lupino. Jerrold Hunter: Alan Marshall. Billy: Terry Kilburn. Sir Ronald Ramsgate: Henry Stephenson. Bassick: Arthur Hohl. Lloyd Brandon: Peter Willes. Justice: Holmes Herbert. Lady Conyngham: Mary Forbes. Stranger: William Austin. Professor Moriarty: George Zucco. Inspector Bristol: E. E. Clive. Mrs Jameson: May Beatty. Mrs Hudson: Mary Gordon.

SHERLOCK HOLMES AND THE VOICE OF TERROR
Universal Pictures   USA   1943
56min. Rel: USA, Sept 1942; GB, 22 Nov 1943.
Dir: John Rawlins. Sherlock Holmes: Basil Rathbone. Dr Watson: Nigel Bruce. Kitty: Evelyn Ankers. Sir Evan Barham: Reginald Denny. Meade:

Thomas Gomez. Anthony Lloyd: Henry Daniell. General Jerome Lawford: Montague Love. Fabian Prentiss: Olaf Hytten. Captain Roland Shore: Leyland Hodgson.
Stated to be based on the story *His Last Bow*.

SHERLOCK HOLMES AND THE SECRET WEAPON
Universal Pictures   USA   1942
68min. Rel: USA, Dec 1942; GB, 2 Jan 1943.
Dir: Roy William Neill. Sc: Edward T. Lowe, W. Scott Darling, Edmund L. Hartmann. Sherlock Holmes: Basil Rathbone. Dr Watson: Nigel Bruce. Charlotte: Kaaren Verne. Professor Moriarty: Lionel Atwill. Inspector Lestrade: Dennis Hoey. Peg Leg: Harold de Becker. Dr Hans Tobel: William Post Jnr. Mrs Hudson: Mary Gordon.

SHERLOCK HOLMES IN WASHINGTON
Universal Pictures   USA   1942
6430ft. Rel: USA, March 1943; GB, 8 Feb 1943.
Dir: Roy William Neill. Sherlock Holmes: Basil Rathbone. Dr Watson: Nigel Bruce. Nancy Partridge: Marjorie Lord. William Easter: Henry Daniell. Stanley: George Zucco. Lieutenant Pete Merriam: John Archer. John Grayson: Gavin Muir. Det Lieut Grogan: Edmund MacDonald.

SHERLOCK HOLMES FACES DEATH
Universal Pictures   USA   1943
68min. Rel: USA, Sept 1943; GB, 10 Apr 1944.
Dir: Roy William Neill. Sc: Bertram Millhauser. Sherlock Holmes: Basil Rathbone. Dr Watson: Nigel Bruce. Inspector Lestrade: Dennis Hoey. Doctor Sexton: Arthur Margetson. Sally Musgrave: Hillary Brooke. Brunton: Halliwell Hobbes. Mrs Howells: Minna Phillips. Captain Vickery: Milburn Stone. Phillip Musgrave: Gavin Muir. Geoffrey Musgrave: Frederick Worlock. Mrs Hudson: Mary Gordon.
Based on *The Musgrave Ritual*.

SPIDER WOMAN
Universal Pictures   USA   1944
5606ft. Rel: USA, Jan 1944; GB, 8 May 1944.
Dir and Prod: Roy William Neill. Sc: Bertram Millhauser. Sherlock Holmes: Basil Rathbone. Dr Watson: Nigel Bruce. Adrea Spenning: Gale Sondergaard. Inspector Lestrade: Dennis Hoey. Mrs Hudson: Mary Gordon.

THE SCARLET CLAW
Universal Pictures   USA   1944
6657ft. Rel: USA, June 1944; GB, 18 Sept 1944.
Dir: Roy William Neill. Sherlock Holmes: Basil Rathbone. Dr Watson:

Nigel Bruce. Potts, Tanner and Ramson: Gerald Hamer. Lord Penrose: Paul Cavanagh. Emile Journet: Arthur Hohl. Judge Brisson: Miles Mander.

THE PEARL OF DEATH
Universal Pictures   USA   1944
6184ft. Rel: USA, Aug 1944; GB, 19 Feb 1945.
Dir and Prod: Roy William Neill. Sc: Bertram Millhauser. Sherlock Holmes: Basil Rathbone. Dr Watson: Nigel Bruce. Inspector Lestrade: Dennis Hoey. Naomi Drake: Evelyn Ankers. Giles Conover: Miles Mander. Mrs Hudson: Mary Gordon. The Creeper: Rondo Hatton.
Based on *The Six Napoleons*.

THE HOUSE OF FEAR
Universal Pictures   USA   1945
5986ft. Rel: USA, March 1945; GB, 9 July 1945.
Dir and Prod: Roy William Neill. Sc: Roy Chanslor. Sherlock Holmes: Basil Rathbone. Dr Watson: Nigel Bruce. Bruce Alastair: Aubrey Mather. Inspector Lestrade: Dennis Hoey. Simon Merrivale: Paul Cavanagh.
Based on *The Five Orange Pips*.

THE WOMAN IN GREEN
Universal Pictures   USA   1945
6094ft. Rel: USA, June 1945; GB, 20 Aug 1945.
Dir and Prod: Roy William Neill. Sc: Bertram Millhauser. Sherlock Holmes: Basil Rathbone. Dr Watson: Nigel Bruce. Lydia Marlowe: Hillary Brooke. Professor Moriarty: Henry Daniell. Sir George Fenwick: Paul Cavanagh. Inspector Gregson: Matthew Boulton. Mrs Hudson: Mary Gordon.

PURSUIT TO ALGIERS
Universal Pictures   USA   1945
65min. Rel: USA, Oct 1945; GB, 4 Feb 1946.
Dir and Prod: Roy William Neill. Sc: Leonard Lee. Sherlock Holmes: Basil Rathbone. Dr Watson: Nigel Bruce. Sheila: Marjorie Riordan. Agatha Dunham: Rosalind Ivan. Mirko: Martin Kosleck. Prime Minister: Frederick Worlock. Sanford: Morton Lowry.

TERROR BY NIGHT
Universal Pictures   USA   1946
60min. Rel: USA, Feb 1946; GB, 8 June 1946.
Dir and Prod: Roy William Neill. Sc: Frank Gruber. Sherlock Holmes: Basil Rathbone. Dr Watson: Nigel Bruce. Major Duncan-Bleek: Alan Mowbray. Inspector Lestrade: Dennis Hoey. Vivian Ledder: Renee Godfrey. Lady Margaret Carstairs: Mary Forbes. Train attendant: Billy Bevan. Professor Kilbane: Frederick Worlock. Hon Ronald Carstairs: Geoffrey Steele. Inspector MacDonald: Boyd Davis.

DRESSED TO KILL (GB: SHERLOCK HOLMES AND THE SECRET CODE)
Universal Pictures   USA   1946
6477ft. Rel: USA, May 1946; GB, 26 Aug 1946.
Prod and Dir: Roy William Neill. Sc: Leonard Lee. Sherlock Holmes: Basil Rathbone. Dr Watson: Nigel Bruce. Hilda Courtney: Patricia Morison. Gilbert Emery: Edmond Breon. Colonel Cavanagh: Frederic Worlock. Inspector Hopkins: Carl Harbord. Mrs Hudson: Mary Gordon.

SHERLOCK HOLMES SIEHT DEM TOD INS GESICHT
(Sherlock Holmes Faces Death)
Universal Pictures
A German combination of the two Universal films *The Scarlet Claw* and *Spider Woman*, merged to make one film with a dubbed German soundtrack.

SHERLOCK HOLMES JAGT DEN TEUFEL VON SOHO
(Sherlock Holmes Hunts the Soho Devil)
Universal Pictures
A German combination of the two Universal films *Sherlock Holmes Faces Death* and *The Pearl of Death*, merged to make one film with a dubbed German soundtrack.

THE ADVENTURE OF THE SPECKLED BAND
Marshall–Grant–Realm Television Productions   USA   1949
25min. TV film.
Dir: Sobey Martin. Sc: Walter Doniger. Sherlock Holmes: Alan Napier. Dr Watson: Melville Cooper.
In the series *Story Theatre* by ZIV Television.

THE MAN WITH THE TWISTED LIP
Vandyke Pictures   GB   1951
3214ft. Rel: GB, Apr 1951.
Dir: Richard M. Grey. Sherlock Holmes: John Longden. Dr Watson: Campbell Singer. Neville St Clair: Hector Ross. Made as a pilot film for a television series.

SHERLOCK HOLMES

A series of television films, 27min each, made by Guild Films in France in 1954.
Sherlock Holmes: Ronald Howard. Dr Watson: Howard Marion Crawford.

THE CASE OF THE CUNNINGHAM HERITAGE
Dir: Jack Gage. Prod and Sc: Sheldon Reynolds. Inspector Lestrade: Archie Duncan. Mrs Cunningham: Meg Lemonnier. Joan: Ursula Howells. Lord Stamford: Rowland Bartrop. Ralph: Pierre Gay.
The pilot film of the Guild series of TV films.

LADY BERYL
Dir: Jack Gage. Prod: Nicole Milinaire. Sc: Sheldon Reynolds. Lady Beryl: Paulette Goddard. Inspector Lestrade: Archie Duncan. Lord Beryl: Peter Copley. Ross: Duncan Elliot. Bobby: Richard Larke.

THE WINTHROP LEGEND
Dir: Jack Gage. Sc: Harold J. Bloom. Prod: Nicole Milinaire. Harvey Winthrop: Ivan Desny. Alice Winthrop: Meg Lemonnier. John Winthrop: Peter Copley. Peg: Guita Karen. Constable: Charles Perry.

THE MOTHER HUBBARD CASE
Dir: Sheldon Reynolds. Prod: Nicole Milinaire. Sc: Lou Morheim. Inspector Lestrade: Archie Duncan. Frances: Michele Wright. Mrs Enid: Amy Dalby. Richard Trevor: William Millinship. Bartender: Percy Arthur Edwards. Lemannel Withers: Jeane Ozenne. Margaret: Delphine Seyrig. Cookson: Billy Beck. Sergeant: Richard Larke.

THE PENNSYLVANIA GUN
Dir: Sheldon Reynolds. Prod: Nicole Milinaire. Sc: Henry Sandoz. Macleod: Russel Waters. Morelle: Emilio Carver. Sergeant: Frank Dexter. Telegraphist: Nicholas Swarbrick.

THE RED-HEADED LEAGUE
Dir: Sheldon Reynolds. Prod: Nicole Milinaire. Sc: Lou Morheim. Inspector Lestrade: Archie Duncan. Jabez Wilson: Alexander Gauge. Vincent Spaulding: Eugene Deckers. Duncan Ross: Colin Drake. Mr Milford: Richard Fitzgerald. Mr Merryweather: M. Seyford. Iverson: G. Bridgman.

THE BELLIGERENT GHOST
Dir: Sheldon Reynolds. Prod: Nicole Milinaire. Sc: Charles M. Early. Inspector Lestrade: Archie Duncan. Maggie Blake: Gertrude Flynn. Bentham: Lou van Burg. Morgue Attendant: Richard Watson. Bobby: Cecil Brock.

THE THISTLE KILLER

THE SHOELESS ENGINEER

THE SHY BALLERINA
Dir: Sheldon Reynolds. Sc: Charles M. Early. Prod: Nicole Milinaire. Inspector Lestrade: Archie Duncan. Harry Chelton: Geoffrey Addinsell. Sergei Smernoff: Eugene Deckers. Elaine Chelton: Nathalie Schaffer. Olga: Martine Alexis.

THE DEADLY PROPHECY
Dir: Sheldon Reynolds. Prod: Nicole Milinaire. Sc: George and Gertrude Fass. Marie Grande: Nicole Courcel. Henri Carolan: Yves Brainville. Antoine: Stephen Swarbrick. Manelli: Robert le Beal. Dr Dimanche: Jacques François. Mme Soule: Helena Manson. Count Passevant: Maurice Teynac.

THE SPLIT TICKET
Dir: Sheldon Reynolds. Prod: Nicole Milinaire. Sc: Lou Morheim. Brian O'Casey: Harry Towb. Belle Rogers: Margaret Russell. Albert Snow: Colin Drake. Baker: Rowland Bartop.

HARRY CROCKER
Dir: Sheldon Reynolds. Prod: Nicole Milinaire. Sc: Harold J. Bloom. Inspector Lestrade: Archie Duncan. Harry Crocker: Eugene Deckers. Charlie: Harry Towb. Dresser: Gertrude Abrahams. Zaza: Aki Yanai. Morgue attendant: Jacques Hilling.

THE RELUCTANT CARPENTER

THE TEXAS COWGIRL

THE LAUGHING MUMMY

THE DIAMOND TOOTH

BLIND MAN'S BLUFF

THE GREYSTONE INSCRIPTION

THE FRENCH INTERPRETER

THE VANISHED DETECTIVE

THE CARELESS SUFFRAGETTE

THE BAKER STREET NURSEMAIDS

THE TYRANT'S DAUGHTER

THE IMPOSTOR MYSTERY

THE CHRISTMAS PUDDING
Dir: Steve Previn. Prod: Sheldon Reynolds. Sc: George and Gertrude Fass. John Norton: Eugene Deckers. Bess Norton: June Rodney. Governor: Richard Watson.

THE JOLLY HANGMAN

THE IMPROMPTU PERFORMANCE

THE SINGING VIOLIN

THE VIOLENT SUITOR

THE NIGHT TRAIN RIDDLE

THE PERFECT HUSBAND

THE UNLUCKY GAMBLER
Dir: Steve Previn. Sc: Joe Morheim. Inspector Lestrade: Archie Duncan.

Sgt Wilkins: Kenneth Richards. Andrew Fenwick: Richard O'Sullivan. Herbert Fenwick: Rowland Bartrop. Bartender: John Buckmaster.

THE EXHUMED CLIENT

THE NEUROTIC DETECTIVE

THE BAKER STREET BACHELORS

THE EIFFEL TOWER

THE HAUNTED GAINSBOROUGH
Dir: Steve Previn. Sc: Charles and Joseph Early. Malcolm McGuggan: Archie Duncan. Heather: Cleo Rose. McLeish: John Buckmaster. Archie Ross: Zack Metalon. Sam Scott: Roger Garris.

A CASE OF ROYAL MURDER
Dir: Steve Previn. Sc: Charles and Joseph Early. King Conrad: Jacques Dacqumine. Princess Antonia: Lise Bourdin. Count Major: Jacques François. Prince Stephen: Maurice Teynac.

THE HOUND OF THE BASKERVILLES
Hammer Film Productions Ltd   GB   1959
7772ft. 87min. Rel: GB, March 1959. Technicolor.
Dir: Terence Fisher. Sc: Peter Bryan. Sherlock Holmes: Peter Cushing. Dr Watson: Andre Morell. Sir Henry Baskerville: Christopher Lee. Cecile: Marla Landi. Sir Hugo Baskerville: David Oxley. Bishop Frankland: Miles Malleson. Dr Mortimer: Francis De Wolff. Stapleton: Ewen Solon. Barrymore: John Le Mesurier. Perkins: Sam Kydd. Servant girl: Judi Moyens. Mrs Barrymore: Helen Goss.

SHERLOCK HOLMES UND DAS HALSBAND DES TODES (GB: SHERLOCK HOLMES AND THE DEADLY NECKLACE)
CCC Film   West Germany   1962
7710ft. 86min. Rel: GB, 1968.
Dir: Terence Fisher. Sc: Curt Siodmak. Sherlock Holmes: Christopher Lee. Dr Watson: Thorley Walters. Professor Moriarty: Hans Söhnker. Ellen Blackburn: Senta Berger. Inspektor Cooper: Hans Nielson.
Partly based on *The Valley of Fear*.

A STUDY IN TERROR
Compton-Cameo Films   GB   1965
95min. Rel: GB, Nov 1965. Eastmancolour.
Dir: James Hill. Sc: Donald and Derek Ford. Sherlock Holmes: John Neville. Dr Watson: Donald Houston. Lord Carfax: John Fraser. Dr Murray: Anthony Quayle. Mycroft Holmes: Robert Morley. Annie Chapman: Barbara Windsor. Angela: Adrienne Corri. Inspector Lestrade: Frank Finlay. Sally: Judi Dench.

Joseph Beck: Charles Regner. Prime Minister: Cecil Parker. Singer: Georgia Brown. Duke of Shires: Barry Jones. Chunky: Terry Downes. Home Secretary: Dudley Foster. Max Steiner: Peter Carsten. Polly Nicholls: Christine Maybach. Cathy Eddowes: Kay Walsh. Simpleton: John Cairney. Mary Kelly: Edna Ronay. Landlady: Avis Bunnage. Mrs Hudson: Barbara Leake. PC Benson: Patrick Newell. Liz Stride: Norma Foster.
Published as *Sherlock Holmes versus Jack the Ripper* by Ellery Queen, Gollancz (London, 1967).

THE PRIVATE LIFE OF SHERLOCK HOLMES
Mirisch Production Co/United Artists   GB   1970
125min. Rel: USA, 28 Oct 1970; Sweden, 28 Oct 1970; GB, 3 Dec 1970. De Luxe colour.
Prod and Dir: Billy Wilder. Sc: Billy Wilder and I. A. L. Diamond. Sherlock Holmes: Robert Stephens. Dr Watson: Colin Blakely. Mrs Hudson: Irene Handl. 1st Gravedigger: Stanley Holloway. Mycroft Holmes: Christopher Lee. Gabrielle Valladon: Genevieve Page. Rogozhin: Clive Revill. Petrova: Tamara Toumanova. Old Lady: Catherine Lacey. Queen Victoria: Mollie Maureen. Von Tirpitz: Peter Madden.
Published as *The Private Life of Sherlock Holmes* by Michael and Mollie Hardwick, Mayflower (London, 1970).

TOUHA SHERLOCKA HOLMESE (Sherlock Holmes's Desire)
Czechoslovak Film   Czechoslovakia   1971
1090m. Rel: Czech (?) Colour.
Dir: Stepan Skalsky. Sc: Ilja Hurnik, Stepan Skalsky. Sherlock Holmes: Radovan Lukavsky. Dr Watson: Vaclav Voska. Lady Abraham: Vlasta Fialova. Lady Oberon: Marie Rosulkova. Maestro: Bohus Zahorsky. Conductor: Eduard Kohout. Lord Biddleton: Miroslav Machacek. Mr Wrubelski: Vlastimil Brodsky. Sir A. C. Doyle: Josef Patocka.

THEY MIGHT BE GIANTS
Universal   USA   1972
86min. Rel: USA, 1972; GB, March 1972   Technicolor.
Dir: Anthony Harvey. Sc: James Goldman, based on his play. Justin Playfair (Sherlock Holmes): George C. Scott. Dr Mildred Watson: Joanne Woodward, Wilbur Peabody: Jack Gilford. Blevins Playfair: Lester Rawlins.

THE HOUND OF THE BASKERVILLES
American Broadcasting System   USA   1972
TV Film.
First shown 12 Feb 1972; shown on British television 1973. Colour.
Sherlock Holmes: Stewart Granger. Dr Watson: Bernard Fox. Stapleton: William Shatner.

MONSIEUR SHERLOK HOLMES
Production company (?)   France   1974
55min.
TV film based on *The Sign of Four*.
Cast included Rolf Becker, Roger Lumont, Gila von Weitershausen.
Shown on Swedish television as *Sherlock Holmes och Hämnaren*, 26 April 1974.

Comedy and Burlesque Films

THE SLEUTHS SERIES

Dir: Mack Sennett. The Sleuths: Mack Sennett, Fred Mace.
Made by Biograph (B) and Keystone (K).

$500.00 Reward (B)	21 Aug 1911
Trailing the Counterfeiters (B)	12 Oct 1911
Their First Divorce Case (B)	2 Nov 1911
Caught with the Goods (B)	25 Dec 1911
Their First Kidnapping Case (B)	11 Apr 1912
At It Again (K)	4 Nov 1912
A Bear Escape (K)	25 Nov 1912
The Stolen Purse (K)	10 Feb 1913
The Sleuths' Last Stand (K)	3 March 1913
The Sleuths at the Floral Parade (K)	6 March 1913
Their First Execution (K)	15 May 1913

THE OTHERS

Miss Sherlock Holmes	Edison	USA	1908
Gaffes ('Mr. Gaffes is a comic Sherlock Holmes')	Lux	Italy	1909
A Squeedunk Sherlock Holmes	Edison	USA	1909
Detektiv Barock Holmes und sein Hund	Gaumont	France	1909
Hemlock Hoax, the Detective	Lubin	USA	1910
Ein Feiner Streich (A Neat Trick)	Eclipse	France	1911
Fritzchen als Sherlock Holmes	Gaumont	France	1911
Little Sherlock Holmes	Eclair	France	1911
Tweedledum and the Necklace	Ambrosio	Italy	1911
Sherlock Holmes Junior	Rex	USA	1911
A Case for Sherlock Holmes	Cricks & Martin	GB	1911
Charlie Colms and Knave of Spades	Pathe	France	1912
Charlie Colms and the Dancer's Necklace	Pathe	France	1912

The Dandies Club (Charlie Colms)	Pathe	France	1912
A Midget Sherlock Holmes	Pathe	USA	1912
The Pipe (Sherlie Homes)	Vitagraph	USA	1912
Baby Sherlock	Powers	USA	1912
Surelock Jones, Detective	Thanhouser	USA	1912
Dupin and the Stolen Necklace	Urbanova	GB	1912
Mr Whoops, the Detective	Comet	USA	1912
The Flag of Distress (Mr Sherlocko)	Imp	USA	1912
The Kid and the Sleuth	Imp	USA	1912
The Right Clue	Imp	USA	1912
The Robbery at the Railroad Station (Sherlocko and Watso)	Champion	USA	1912
Cousins of Sherlock Holmes	Solax	USA	1913
The Tongue Mark	Majestic	USA	1913
Fricot als Sherlock Holmes	Ambrosio	Italy	1913
The Amateur Sleuth (Herlock Sholmes)	Gaumont	(?)	1913
Homlock Shermes (Pearl, the girl detective)	Crystal	USA	1913
A Would-be Detective	Gem	USA	1913
One on Tooty (Shamlock Bones)	Eclair	(?)	1913
A Canine Sherlock Holmes	Urbanova	GB	1913
Burstup Homes, Detective	Solax	USA	1913
Burstup Homes's Murder Case	Solax	USA	1913
The Case of the Missing Girl	Solax	USA	1913
Moritz Siegt uber Sherlock Holmes (Moritz Triumphs over Sherlock Holmes)	Pathe	France	1914
Gontran als Sherlock Holmes	Eclair	France	1914
Sherlock Bonehead	Kalem	USA	1914
The Sherlock Holmes Girl	Edison	USA	1914
Shorty and Sherlock Holmes	Broncho	USA	1914
A Study in Skarlit	Comedy Combine	GB	1915
Der Floh von Baskerville (The Flea of the Baskervilles)	Luna	Italy	1915
Bloomer Tricks Sherlock Holmes	Cines	Italy	1915
Sherlock Boob, Detective	Mica	USA	1915
A Villainous Villain (Sherlock Oomph)	Vitagraph	USA	1916
A Society Sherlock	Universal	USA	1916
The Great Detective	Kalem	USA	1916
Die Hand	Eiko-Film	Germany	1916
Sherlock Ambrose	L-KO	USA	1918
Sherlock Brown	Metro	USA	1922
Sherlock Jr (Buster Keaton)	Metro-Goldwyn	USA	1924

Sherlock Sleuth	Pathe	USA	1925
Surelock Homes (Felix the Cat)		USA	(?)
Herlock Sholmes in Be-a-Live Crook (Marionette burlesque of Clive Brook's Holmes)	Assoc Sound Films	GB	1930
Sherlock's Home	Vitaphone	USA	1932
The Strange Case of Hennessy (2 reel musical comedy with Silo Dance, a burlesque detective in exaggerated Sherlock Holmes garb)	Van Beuren	USA	1933–4 (?)

Related Films and Grey Areas

UNIVERSAL ANIMATED WEEKLY No 117   3 June 1914
'Creator of Sherlock Holmes – Sir Arthur Conan Doyle visits America for the first time in twenty years, and meets William J. Burns the famous American detective – New York City.'

FOX MOVIETONE   15min   1929
Conan Doyle appeared in a short talking picture and explained how he came to write the Sherlock Holmes stories, and how he was always hearing from the admirers of Holmes throughout the world.

PATHE PICTORIAL No 356   1951
Included *The Sage of Baker Street*, on the Sherlock Holmes Exhibition.

PATHE PICTORIAL No 162   1957
Included 'The Sherlock Holmes Tavern', dealing with the displays in the pub.

PATHE PICTORIAL No 710 (Colour)   1968
The whole of this Pathe Pictorial was devoted to the tour of Switzerland by members of the Sherlock Holmes Society of London.

THE LIFE OF SHERLOCK HOLMES
Slade School of Fine Art   GB   1968
27min.
Dir and Sc: Jeremy Marre.
An amusing biography made as the major project for 1968 by the Film Department of the Slade School. It made extensive use of stills from the London Museum, early newsreel film of London street scenes, and extracts from the Stoll series of silent Sherlock Holmes films featuring Eille Norwood.

MR. SHERLOCK HOLMES OF LONDON
GB   1971
A documentary film for television, first shown 15 Nov 1971. Written and directed by William Taylor. Featuring Anthony Howlett, Dr Maurice Camp-

bell, Bernard Davies, Guy Warrack and other members of the Sherlock Holmes Society of London.

GREY AREAS

CAUGHT
Vitagraph   USA   1907

'*Caught* is apparently founded on one of the Sherlock Holmes stories of A. Conan Doyle.' *Kinematograph Weekly* (20 Feb 1908). There is no 'apparently' about it. The plot is a deliberate crib of *The Red-Headed League* with the police substituted for Sherlock Holmes.

THE HYPNOTIC DETECTIVE   1912

At last we have a chance to meet our old friend Mr. Sherlock Holmes, of Upper Baker Street, in the moving pictures. The fact, however, that he appears under the name of Professor Locksley, that he sports a long moustache and carries a monocle, leads to the grave suspicion that the presentation has not been authorised either by Sir Arthur Conan Doyle or by the publishers of his books. Be that as it may, *The Hypnotic Detective* is in every incident *The Adventure of the Norwood Builder*.

The Bookman (Oct 1912)

VERRATER ZIGARETTE (The Treacherous Cigarette)
SCHWARZE KAPPE (The Black Hood)
These two titles, with the name Sherlock Holmes alongside them, were advertised in *Der Kinematograph* for four consecutive weeks in July 1913. Nothing else known.

THE LOST SPECIAL
Universal   USA   1932
Long regarded by many enthusiasts as a Holmes story that just happens to omit Holmes, this tale by Conan Doyle was used by Universal as the basis of a twelve-part serial.

Commercial Films

1966   Farmer's Wife Double Devon Cream.
TV commercial for Unigate Dairy Sales, made by Clifford Bloxham & Partners Ltd.

1970   Two colour TV commercials for Esso domestic heating oil, made for use on Canadian TV. Each commercial was made in two versions, English and French, with different actors as Sherlock Holmes and Dr Watson.

1972   Carlsberg Lager
Colour TV commercial, made by Rupert Chetwynd & Partners Ltd.
Sherlock Holmes: John Keston. Dr Watson: Raymond Mason.

1972   *The Case of the Metal Sheathed Elements*
16mm colour commercial film, 17min, produced by the Larkins Studio for The Electricity Council.
Cartoon film depiction of Sherlock Holmes and Dr Watson, in an instructional film.
Sherlock Holmes: Frank Duncan. Dr Watson: Norman Bird.

Sherlock Holmes on Radio

THE ADVENTURES OF SHERLOCK HOLMES   USA
WEAF-NBC, 20 Oct 1930–15 June 1931. 35 broadcasts.
Written by Edith Meiser.
This first radio series was launched with William Gillette as Sherlock Holmes,
but only for the first broadcast. Richard Gordon completed the series as Holmes,
with Leigh Lovell as Dr Watson.

20 Oct	*The Speckled Band*
27 Oct	*A Scandal in Bohemia*
3 Nov	*The Red-Headed League*
10 Nov	*The Copper Beeches*
17 Nov	*The Boscombe Valley Mystery*
24 Nov	*The Man with the Twisted Lip*
1 Dec	*The Stockbroker's Clerk*
8 Dec	*Silver Blaze*
15 Dec	*The Crooked Man*
22 Dec	*The Noble Bachelor*
29 Dec	*The Reigate Squires*
5 Jan	*The Musgrave Ritual*
12 Jan	*The Resident Patient*
19 Jan	*The Naval Treaty*
26 Jan	*The Greek Interpreter*
2 Feb	*The Creeping Man*
9 Feb	*The Mazarin Stone*
16 Feb	*The Sussex Vampire*
23 Feb	*The Illustrious Client*
2 March	*The Blanched Soldier*
9 March	*The Five Orange Pips*
16 March	*Thor Bridge*
23 March	*The Lion's Mane*
30 March	*Shoscombe Old Place*
6 Apr	*The Retired Colourman*
13 Apr	*The Norwood Builder*

20 Apr	*The Dancing Men*
27 Apr	*The Solitary Cyclist*
4 May	*The Priory School*
11 May	*Black Peter*
18 May	*Charles Augustus Milverton*
25 May	*The Six Napoleons*
1 June	*The Golden Pince-Nez*
8 June	*The Missing Three-Quarter*
15 June	*Abbey Grange*

THE ADVENTURES OF SHERLOCK HOLMES   USA

WEAF-NBC, 17 Sept–17 Dec 1931; W JZ-NBC, 30 Dec 1931–27 Apr 1932;
WEAF-NBC, 5 May–23 June 1932. 40 broadcasts.
Written by Edith Meiser.
Sherlock Holmes: Richard Gordon. Dr Watson: Leigh Lovell.

17 Sept	(?)
24 Sept	*Lady Frances Carfax*
1 Oct	*Wisteria Lodge*
8 Oct	*The Devil's Foot*
15 Oct	*The Red Circle*
22 Oct	*The Bruce-Partington Plans*
29 Oct	*The Dying Detective*
5 Nov	*The Cardboard Box*
12 Nov	*The Three Gables*
19 Nov–	
10 Dec	*A Study in Scarlet* (Parts 1–4)
17 Dec	*The Engineer's Thumb*
30 Dec	*The Hindoo in the Wicker Basket*
6 Jan	*The Yellow Face*
13 Jan	*The Gloria Scott*
20 Jan	*The Beryl Coronet*
27 Jan–	
2 March	*The Hound of the Baskervilles* (Parts 1–6)
9 March	*Murder in the Waxworks*
16 March	*A Case of Identity*
23 March	*The Ace of Spades*
30 March	*The Missing Leonardo da Vinci*
6 Apr	*The Veiled Lodger*
13 Apr	*The Three Garridebs*
20 Apr	*The Giant Rat of Sumatra*
27 Apr	*The Haunted Clock*
5 May–	
23 June	(?)

THE ADVENTURES OF SHERLOCK HOLMES   USA
WJZ-NBC, 28 Sept 1932–31 May 1933. 36 broadcasts.
Written by Edith Meiser.
Sherlock Holmes: Richard Gordon. Dr Watson: Leigh Lovell.

28 Sept	*The Second Stain*
5 Oct	*The Empty House*
12 Oct	*His Last Bow*
19 Oct	*The Three Students*
26 Oct–	
30 Nov	*The Sign of Four* (Parts 1–6)
7 Dec	*The Blue Carbuncle*
14 Dec	*Death in the Club Window*
21 Dec	*The Haunted Bagpipes*
28 Dec	*Murder by Proxy*
4 Jan	*The Dying Rosebush*
11 Jan	*The Missing Black Bag*
18 Jan	*Her Majesty's Wine-Cellar*
25 Jan	*The Missing Dancer*
1 Feb	*Death at Stonehenge*
8 Feb	*Mr Pottle's Secret Profession*
15 Feb	*The Voodoo Curse*
22 Feb	*Death Holds the Prompt Book*
1 March	*The Typewritten Will*
8 March	*The Aristocratic Model*
15 March	*The Poison Keg*
22 March	*The Corpse in the Cab*
29 March	*The Jewish Breastplate*
5 Apr	*The Lost Train*
12 Apr	*Shoscombe Old Place*
19 Apr	*The Sealed Room*
26 Apr	*Vamberry, the Wine Merchant*
3 May	*The Walking Corpse*
10 May	*The Poisoned Stick*
17 May	*The Case with Two Solutions*
24 May	*The Singular Affair of the Aluminium Crutch*
31 May	*The Armchair Solution*

THE ADVENTURES OF SHERLOCK HOLMES   USA
WJZ-NBC, 11 Nov 1934–26 May 1935. 29 broadcasts.
Written by Edith Meiser.
Sherlock Holmes: Louis Hector. Dr Watson: Leigh Lovell.

11 Nov	*The Jewish Breastplate*
18 Nov	*The Lost Special*

25 Nov	*The Syrian Mummy*
2 Dec	*The Sealed Room*
9 Dec	*Vamberry, the Wine Merchant*
16 Dec	(?)
23 Dec	*The Poisoned Stick*
30 Dec	(?)
6 Jan	(?)
13 Jan	*The Armchair Solution*
20 Jan	*The Dual Personality*
27 Jan	(?)
3 Feb	*Cherchez la Femme*
10 Feb–	
26 May	(?)

SHERLOCK HOLMES   USA
WABC, 18 Nov 1935.
In the series Lux Radio Theatre. Written by Edith Meiser, from the stage play by William Gillette.
Sherlock Holmes: William Gillette. Dr Watson: Reginald Mason. Alice Faulkner: Betty Hanna. James Larrabee: Reynolds Denniston. Sid Prince: William Postance. Professor Moriarty: Charles Bryant.

SHERLOCK HOLMES   USA
WOR-MBS, 1 Feb–26 Sept; WEAF-NBC, 1 Oct–24 Dec 1936. 48 broadcasts.
Written by Edith Meiser.
Sherlock Holmes: Richard Gordon. Dr Watson: Harry West.

1 Feb	*The Speckled Band*
8 Feb	*The Red-Headed League*
15 Feb	*A Scandal in Bohemia*
22 Feb	*The Man with the Twisted Lip*
29 Feb	*The Reigate Squires*
7 March	*The Sussex Vampire*
14 March	*The Resident Patient*
21 March	*The Creeping Man*
28 March	*The Dying Detective*
4 Apr	*The Hindoo in the Wicker Basket*
11 Apr	*Silver Blaze*
18 Apr	*The Illustrious Client*
25 Apr	*Death in the Club Window*
2 May	*The Blanched Soldier*
9 May	*The Dancing Men*
16 May	*Death at Stonehenge*
23 May	*The Mazarin Stone*

30 May	*The Devil's Foot*
6 June	*The Armchair Solution*
13 June	*Thor Bridge*
20 June	*The Solitary Cyclist*
27 June	*The Musgrave Ritual*
4 July	*The Typewritten Will*
11 July	*The Stockbroker's Clerk*
18 July	*The Giant Rat of Sumatra*
25 July	*The Noble Bachelor*
1 Aug	*The Lion's Mane*
8 Aug	*The Norwood Builder*
15 Aug	*The Naval Treaty*
22 Aug	*Murder in the Waxworks*
29 Aug	*A Scandal in Bohemia*
5 Sept	(?)
12 Sept	*The Missing Three-Quarter*
19 Sept	*The Beryl Coronet*
26 Sept	*Wisteria Lodge*
1 Oct	*The Sealed Room*
8 Oct	*The Voodoo Curse*
15 Oct	*The Empty House*
22 Oct	*The Haunted Bagpipes*
29 Oct	*The Dying Rosebush*
5 Nov	(?)
12 Nov	*The Second Stain*
19 Nov	*The Golden Pince-Nez*
26 Nov	*Black Peter*
3 Dec	*The Six Napoleons*
10 Dec	*The Retired Colourman*
17 Dec	*The Cardboard Box*
24 Dec	*The Blue Carbuncle*

SHERLOCK HOLMES   USA
WABC-CBS, 25 Sept 1938.
In the series Mercury Theatre on the Air. Written by Orson Welles from the stage play by William Gillette.
Sherlock Holmes: Orson Welles. Dr Watson: Ray Collins.

THE ADVENTURES OF SHERLOCK HOLMES   USA
WJZ-NBC, 2 Oct 1939–11 March 1940. 24 broadcasts.
Written by Edith Meiser. Produced by Harold Kemp.
Sherlock Holmes: Basil Rathbone. Dr Watson: Nigel Bruce.

| 2 Oct | *The Sussex Vampire* |

9 Oct	*Silver Blaze*
16 Oct	*The Speckled Band*
23 Oct	*The Man with the Twisted Lip*
30 Oct	*The Devil's Foot*
6 Nov	*The Bruce-Partington Plans*
13 Nov	*The Lion's Mane*
20 Nov	*The Dying Detective*
27 Nov	*The Creeping Man*
4 Dec	*Charles Augustus Milverton*
11 Dec	*The Musgrave Ritual*
18 Dec	*Wisteria Lodge*
25 Dec	*The Three Garridebs*
1 Jan	*The Blue Carbuncle*
8 Jan	*The Priory School*
15 Jan	*The Greek Interpreter*
22 Jan	*The Cardboard Box*
29 Jan	*The Second Stain*
5 Feb	*Abbey Grange*
12 Feb	*Shoscombe Old Place*
19 Feb	*The Blanched Soldier*
26 Feb	*The Reigate Squires*
4 March	*The Beryl Coronet*
11 March	*The Retired Colourman*

SHERLOCK HOLMES   USA

WJZ–NBC, 29 Sept 1940–9 March 1941. 24 broadcasts.
Written by Edith Meiser. Produced by Tom McKnight.
Sherlock Holmes: Basil Rathbone. Dr Watson: Nigel Bruce.

29 Sept	*The Empty House*
6 Oct	*The Copper Beeches*
13 Oct	*The Noble Bachelor*
20 Oct	*The Engineer's Thumb*
27 Oct	*The Red-Headed League*
3 Nov	*Thor Bridge*
10 Nov	*The Crooked Man*
17 Nov	*The Norwood Hills Mystery*
24 Nov	*The Three Students*
1 Dec	*The Dancing Men*
8 Dec	*Black Peter*
15 Dec	*The Lost Naval Treaty*
22 Dec	*The Boscombe Valley Mystery*
29 Dec	*The Missing Three-Quarter*
5 Jan	*The Mazarin Stone*

12 Jan–	
16 Feb	*The Hound of the Baskervilles* (Parts 1–6)
23 Feb	*The Resident Patient*
2 March	*The Speckled Band*
9 March	*Shoscombe Old Place*

SHERLOCK HOLMES   USA
WEAF-NBC, 5 Oct 1941–1 March 1942. 22 broadcasts.
Written by Edith Meiser. Produced by Russell Seeds.
Sherlock Holmes: Basil Rathbone. Dr Watson: Nigel Bruce.

5 Oct	*The Illustrious Client*
12 Oct	*The Six Napoleons*
19 Oct	*The Devil's Foot*
26 Oct	*The Solitary Cyclist*
2 Nov	*The Walking Corpse*
9 Nov	*The Stockbroker's Clerk*
16 Nov	*The Missing Papers*
23 Nov	*The Magician*
30 Nov	*A Case of Identity*
7 Dec	*Mrs Warren's Key*
14 Dec	*The Dark Gentleman*
21 Dec	*Donald's Death*
28 Dec	*The Gloria Scott*
4 Jan	*The Second Stain*
11 Jan	*The Haunted Bagpipes*
18 Jan	*The Three Gables*
25 Jan	*The Lion's Mane*
1 Feb	*The Five Orange Pips*
8 Feb	*The Voodoo Curse*
15 Feb	*The Dark Tragedy of the Circus*
22 Feb	*The Sussex Vampire*
1 March	*The Giant Rat of Sumatra*

SHERLOCK HOLMES   USA
WOR-MBS, 30 Apr–1 Oct 1943. 23 broadcasts.
Written by Edith Meiser. Directed by Glenn Heisch.
Sherlock Holmes: Basil Rathbone. Dr Watson: Nigel Bruce.

30 Apr	(?)
7 May	*The Copper Beeches*
14 May	*The Man with the Twisted Lip*
21 May	*The Devil's Foot*
28 May	*The Red-Headed League*
4 June	*The Engineer's Thumb*

11 June	*Silver Blaze*
18 June	*The Dying Detective*
25 June	*Wisteria Lodge*
2 July	*The Priory School*
9 July	*The Creeping Man*
16 July	*The Musgrave Ritual*
23 July	*The Greek Interpreter*
30 July	*Murder in the Waxworks*
6 Aug	*The Missing Leonardo da Vinci*
13 Aug	*The Syrian Mummy*
20 Aug	*The Missing Dancer*
27 Aug	*The Cardboard Box*
3 Sept	*The Retired Colourman*
10 Sept	*The Bruce-Partington Plans*
17 Sept	*The Dying Rosebush*
24 Sept	*The Missing Black Bag*
1 Oct	*The Speckled Band*

THE BOSCOMBE VALLEY MYSTERY
BBC Home Service, 3 July 1943.
In the series Saturday Night Theatre.
Written by Ashley Sampson. Produced by Howard Rose.
Sherlock Holmes: Arthur Wontner. Dr Watson: Carleton Hobbs

MY DEAR WATSON
BBC Home Service, July 1943.
A biography of John H. Watson, MD.
No writer credited. Produced by Francis Dillon.
Sherlock Holmes: John Cheatle. Dr Watson: Ralph Truman.

SHERLOCK HOLMES   USA
WOR-MBS, 4 Oct 1943–28 May 1945. 87 broadcasts.
Written by Bruce Taylor (Leslie Charteris), Denis Green and Anthony Boucher.
Produced by Glenhall Taylor.
Sherlock Holmes: Basil Rathbone. Dr Watson: Nigel Bruce.

4 Oct	(?)
11 Oct	(?)
18 Oct	(?)
25 Oct	*Ricoletti of the Club Foot*
1 Nov	*The Brother's Footsteps*
8 Nov	*The Shocking Affair of the SS Friesland*
15 Nov	*The Apparition at Sadler's Wells*
22 Nov	*Murder at the Park*

29 Nov	*Mrs Farintosh's Opal Tiara*
6 Dec	*The Camberwell Poisoning Case*
13 Dec	*The Jumping Jack*
20 Dec	*The Missing Black Dog*
27 Dec	*The Tired Captain*
3 Jan	(?)
10 Jan	(?)
17 Jan	*The Departed Banker*
24 Jan	*The Amateur Mendicant Society*
31 Jan	*The Dog that Howled in the Night*
7 Feb	*Death at Cornwall*
14 Feb	*The Red Leeches*
21 Feb	*Dr Moore Agar*
28 Feb	*The Missing Bullion*
6 March	*Death on the Scottish Express*
13 March	*The Peculiar Persecution of John Vincent Hardin*
20 March	*The Man who Drowned in Paddington Station*
27 March	*The Haunted Bagpipes*
3 Apr	*The Fingerprints that Couldn't Lie*
10 Apr	*The Man who Was Hanged*
17 Apr	*The Singular Contents of the Ancient British Barrow*
24 Apr	*The Dentist who Used Wolfbane*
1 May	*Holmes and the Half Man*
8 May	*The Phantom Iceberg*
15 May	*The Missing Bloodstains*
22 May	*The Superfluous Pearl*
29 May	*Skull and Bones*
5 June	*The Corpse in a Trunk*
12 June	*The Monster of Gyre*
19 June	*The Man with the Twisted Lip*
26 June	*The Dissimilar Body*
3 July	*The Amateur Mendicant Society*
10 July	*The Devil's Foot*
17 July	*The Bruce-Partington Plans*
24 July	*The Strange Case of the Aluminium Crutch*
31 July	*The Giant Rat of Sumatra*
7 Aug	*The Lighthouse, the Frightened Politician and the Trained Cormorant*
14 Aug	*Murder by Remote Control*
21 Aug	*The Missing Corpse*
28 Aug	*The African Leopard Man*
4 Sept	*Dimitrios, the Divine*
11 Sept	*Guardian of the Dead*
18 Sept	*The Invisible Necklace*
25 Sept	*The Vampire of Cadiz*

2 Oct	*200 Year-Old Murderer*
9 Oct	*The Third Hunchback*
16 Oct	*The Missing Treaty*
23 Oct	*League of Unhappy Orphans*
30 Oct	*The Haunted Chateau*
6 Nov	*Murder under the Big Top*
13 Nov	*The Strange Case of the Veiled Horseman*
20 Nov	*The Secret of Glaive*
27 Nov	*The Steamship Friesland*
4 Dec	*The Telltale Bruises*
11 Dec	*The Island of Uffa*
18 Dec	*The Wandering Miser*
25 Dec	*The Blue Carbuncle*
1 Jan	*Should Auld Acquaintance Be Forgot?*
8 Jan	*The Play's the Thing*
15 Jan	*Dr Anselmo*
22 Jan	*The Elusive Umbrella*
29 Jan	*The Werewolf of Vair*
5 Feb	*The Dead Adventuress*
12 Feb	*The Newmarket Killers*
19 Feb	*The Surrey Inn*
26 Feb	*Lady Frances Carfax*
5 March	*The Doomed Sextet*
12 March	*The Erratic Windmill*
19 March	*The Secret of Stonehenge*
26 March	*The Book of Tobit*
2 Apr	*The Amateur Mendicant Society*
9 Apr	*The Viennese Strangler*
16 Apr	*The Remarkable Worm*
23 Apr	*The Notorious Canary Trainer*
30 Apr	*The Unfortunate Tobacconist*
7 May	*The Purloined Ruby*
14 May	*On the Flanders*
21 May	*The Paradol Chamber*
28 May	*Dance of Death*

SHERLOCK HOLMES AND DR WATSON
BBC Home Service, 18 Apr 1944.
Demonstration programme for schools. Sherlock Holmes: Carleton Hobbs.

HAVE YOU READ THE ADVENTURES OF SHERLOCK HOLMES?
BBC London Transcription Service, 19 May 1945.
Sherlock Holmes: Carleton Hobbs.

THE ADVENTURE OF THE SPECKLED BAND
BBC Home Service, 17 May 1945.
Written by John Dickson Carr. Produced by Martyn C. Webster.
Introduced by Adrian Conan Doyle.
Sherlock Holmes: Sir Cedric Hardwicke. Dr. Watson: Finlay Currie.

SILVER BLAZE
BBC Home Service, 9 Aug 1945.
In the series 'Corner in Crime'. Written by C. Gordon Glover. Produced by
Walter Rilla.
Sherlock Holmes: Laidman Browne. Dr Watson: Norman Shelley.

SHERLOCK HOLMES   USA
WOR–MBS, 3 Sept 1945–27 May 1946. 38 broadcasts.
Written by Denis Green and Anthony Boucher. Produced by Edna Best.
Sherlock Holmes: Basil Rathbone. Dr Watson: Nigel Bruce.

3 Sept	*The Limping Ghost*
10 Sept	*Col Warburton's Madness*
17 Sept	*Out of Date Murder*
24 Sept	*The Eyes of Mr Leyton*
1 Oct	*Thor Bridge*
8 Oct	*The Vanishing Elephant*
15 Oct	*The Manor House Case*
22 Oct	*The Great Gandolfo*
29 Oct	*Murder by Moonlight*
5 Nov	*The Fifth of November*
12 Nov	*The Speckled Band*
19 Nov	*The Double Zero*
26 Nov	*The Accidental Murderess*
3 Dec	*Murder in the Casbah*
10 Dec	*A Scandal in Bohemia*
17 Dec	*The Daughter of Irene Adler*
24 Dec	*The Night before Christmas*
31 Dec	*The Strange Case of the Iron Box*
7 Jan	*The Hampton Heath Killer*
14 Jan	*Murder in the Himalayas*
21 Jan	*The Telltale Pigeon Feathers*
28 Jan	*Sweeney Todd, the Demon Barber*
4 Feb	*The Cross of Damascus*
11 Feb	(?)
18 Feb	*The Camberwell Poisoning Case*
25 Feb	*Murder at the Opera*
4 March	(?)

11 March	*The Living Doll*
18 March	*The Blarney Stone*
25 March	*The Girl with the Gazelle*
1 Apr	*The April Fool's Adventure*
8 Apr	*The Vanishing Scientists*
15 Apr	(?)
22 Apr	(?)
29 Apr	*Waltz of Death*
6 May	*The Man with the Twisted Lip*
13 May	*The Uneasy Chair*
20 May	*The Haunting of Sherlock Holmes*
27 May	*The Singular Affair of the Baconian Cipher*

THE NEW ADVENTURES OF SHERLOCK HOLMES USA

WJZ-ABC, 12 Oct 1946–7 July 1947. 39 broadcasts.
Written by Anthony Boucher and Denis Green. Produced by Tom McKnight.
Sherlock Holmes: Tom Conway. Dr Watson: Nigel Bruce.

12 Oct	(?)
19 Oct	*The Black Angus*
26 Oct	*The Clue of the Hungry Cat*
2 Nov	(?)
9 Nov	(?)
16 Nov	*The Murdered Violinist*
23 Nov	(?)
30 Nov	*The Strange Death of Mrs Abernetty*
7 Dec	*The Coptic Compass*
14 Dec	*The Vanishing Emerald*
21 Dec	(?)
28 Dec	*The White Cockerel*
4 Jan	(?)
13 Jan	(?)
20 Jan	*The Babbling Butler*
27 Jan	(?)
3 Feb	*The Dying Detective*
10 Feb	*The Persecuted Millionaire*
17 Feb	*The Haunted Bagpipes*
24 Feb	*The Horseless Carriage*
3 March	*Queue for Murder*
10 March	*The Egyptian Curse*
17 March	(?)
24 March	*The Scarlet Worm*
31 March	(?)
7 Apr	(?)

14 Apr	*The Carpathian Horror*
21 Apr	(?)
28 Apr	*The Island of Death*
5 May	*The Pointless Robbery*
12 May	*The Voodoo Curse*
19 May	(?)
26 May	*A Submerged Baronet*
2 June	*The Red-Headed League*
9 June	(?)
16 June	(?)
23 June	*The Speckled Band*
30 June	(?)
7 July	(?)

HAVE YOU MET SHERLOCK HOLMES?

BBC Home Service, 7 Feb 1947. Schools broadcasts – Senior English.
Sherlock Holmes: Carleton Hobbs.

SHERLOCK HOLMES   USA

WOR-MBS, 28 Sept 1947–20 June 1948. 39 broadcasts.
Written by Edith Meiser. Produced by Basil Loughrane.
Sherlock Holmes: John Stanley. Dr Watson: Alfred Shirley

28 Sept	*The Dog who Changed his Mind*
5 Oct	*The Missing Heiress*
12 Oct	*The Red-Headed League*
19 Oct	*The Affair of the Politician, the Lighthouse and the Trained Cormorant*
26 Oct	*The Laughing Lemur of Hightower Heath*
2 Nov	*The Copper Beeches*
9 Nov	*The Cadaver in the Roman Toga*
16 Nov	*The Well-Staged Murder*
23 Nov	*The Stolen Naval Treaty*
30 Nov	*The Cradle that Rocked Itself*
7 Dec	*Professor Moriarty and the Diamond Jubilee*
14 Dec	*The Sussex Vampire*
21 Dec	*The Christmas Bride*
28 Dec	*New Year's Eve Off the Scilly Isles*
4 Jan	*The Mazarin Stone*
11 Jan	*Sudden Senility*
18 Jan	*The Lucky Shilling*
25 Jan	*The Engineer's Thumb*
1 Feb	*The Avenging Blade*
8 Feb	*The Sanguinary Specter*
15 Feb	*Shoscombe Old Place*

22 Feb	*The Wooden Claw*
29 Feb	*King Philip's Golden Salver*
7 March	*The Six Napoleons*
14 March	*The Serpent God*
21 March	*Death Is a Golden Arrow*
28 March	*Lady Frances Carfax*
4 Apr	*The Return of the Monster*
11 Apr	(?)
18 Apr	*The Very Best Butter*
25 Apr	*The Return of the Jack of Diamonds*
2 May	(?)
9 May	(?)
16 May	*The Everblooming Roses*
23 May	*The Accommodating Valise*
30 May	*A Case of Identity*
6 June	*The Complicated Poisoning at Eel Pie Island*
13 June	(?)
20 June	*The Veiled Lodger*

SHERLOCK HOLMES USA

WOR-MBS, 12 Sept 1948–6 June 1949. 39 broadcasts.
Written by Howard Merrill and others. Produced by Basil Loughrane.
Sherlock Holmes: John Stanley. Dr Watson: Ian Martin.

12 Sept	*The Unwelcome Ambassador*
19 Sept	*The Black Guardsman of Braddock Castle*
26 Sept	(?)
3 Oct	(?)
10 Oct	*The Guy Fawkes Society*
17 Oct	*Black Peter*
24 Oct	(?)
31 Oct	*The Uddington Witch*
7 Nov	*The Logic of Murder*
14 Nov	*The Ancient Queen*
21 Nov	(?)
28 Nov	(?)
5 Dec	*Island of the Dead*
12 Dec	*London Tower*
19 Dec	(?)
26 Dec	*The Blue Carbuncle*
3 Jan	*The Malicious Moor*
10 Jan	*The Knife of Vengeance*
17 Jan	*The Fabulous Celebrities*
24 Jan	*The Guest in the Coffin*

31 Jan	*The Devil's Foot*
7 Feb	*The Blood-stained Goddess*
14 Feb	*The Guest in the Coffin*
21 Feb	(?)
28 Feb	*The East End Strangler*
7 March	*Murder on a Wager*
14 March	*The Unfortunate Valet*
21 March–	
4 Apr	*The Elusive Agent* (Parts 1–3)
11 Apr	*The Mad Miners of Cardiff*
18 Apr	*The Burmese Goddess*
25 Apr	*The Golden Pince-Nez*
2 May	*The Blood-soaked Wagon*
9 May	(?)
16 May	*The Gray Pasha*
23 May	*Dr Winthrop's Notorious Carriage*
30 May	(?)
6 June	(?)

THE ADVENTURE OF THE SPECKLED BAND
BBC Home Service, 26 Dec 1948.
Written by John Dickson Carr. Produced by David H. Godfrey. Introduced by
Adrian Conan Doyle.
Sherlock Holmes: Howard Marion-Crawford. Dr Watson: Finlay Currie.

THE ADVENTURES OF SHERLOCK HOLMES   USA
WJZ-ABC, 21 Sept 1949–14 June 1950. 39 broadcasts.
Written by Denis Green. Produced by Ted Bliss and Ken Manson.
Sherlock Holmes: Ben Wright. Dr Watson: Eric Snowden.
(Titles not known.)

THE SPECKLED BAND
BBC Home Service, 3 Oct 1949. Schools broadcasts – Senior English.
Sherlock Holmes: Carleton Hobbs.

THE RED-HEADED LEAGUE
BBC Home Service, 18 Sept 1950. Schools broadcasts – Senior English.
Sherlock Holmes: Carleton Hobbs.

SHERLOCK HOLMES STORIES
BBC Home Service, 15 Oct 1952–4 Feb 1953.
In Children's Hour. Written by Felix Felton.
Sherlock Holmes: Carleton Hobbs. Dr Watson: Norman Shelley.

15 Oct	*The Naval Treaty*
12 Nov	*The Five Orange Pips*
10 Dec	*The Blue Carbuncle*
7 Jan	*The Red-Headed League*
4 Feb	*The Three Students*

SHERLOCK HOLMES

BBC Home Service, 3 Jan 1953.

In the series Saturday Night Theatre. Repeated 8 Jan 1953.

Written and produced by Raymond Raikes from William Gillette's stage play.

Sherlock Holmes: Carleton Hobbs. Dr Watson: Norman Shelley. Professor Robert Moriarty: Frederick Valk.

At noon on the day of this broadcast, ex-Chief Inspector Fabian of Scotland Yard unveiled a plaque outside the Criterion Restaurant, Piccadilly Circus, commemorating the meeting there of Dr Watson and Dr Stamford that led to the introduction of Dr Watson to Sherlock Holmes. Carleton Hobbs, in Sherlock Holmes attire, arrived in Piccadilly Circus in a hansom cab to attend the ceremony.

TRIBUTE TO SHERLOCK HOLMES

BBC Home Service, 8 Jan 1954.

Written by C. A. Lejeune, R. J. B. Sellar and Norman Claridge.

Sherlock Holmes: Alan Wheatley.

THE ADVENTURES OF SHERLOCK HOLMES

BBC Light Programme, 5 Oct–21 Dec 1954.

A Harry Alan Towers Production. Written by John Keir Cross.

Sherlock Holmes: John Gielgud. Dr Watson: Ralph Richardson. Professor Moriarty: Orson Welles.

5 Oct	*Dr Watson Meets Sherlock Holmes*
	(The beginning of *A Study in Scarlet*, plus *Charles Augustus Milverton*)
12 Oct	*A Scandal in Bohemia*
19 Oct	*The Red-Headed League*
26 Oct	*The Bruce-Partington Plans*
2 Nov	*A Case of Identity*
9 Nov	*The Dying Detective*
16 Nov	*The Second Stain*
23 Nov	*The Norwood Builder*
30 Nov	*The Solitary Cyclist*
7 Dec	*The Six Napoleons*
14 Dec	*The Blue Carbuncle*
21 Dec	*The Final Problem*

SHERLOCK HOLMES STORIES
BBC Home Service, 7 Oct 1954–3 March 1955.
In Children's Hour. Written by Felix Felton.
Sherlock Holmes: Carleton Hobbs. Dr Watson: Norman Shelley. Inspector Lestrade: Felix Felton.

7 Oct	*The Norwood Builder*
4 Nov	*The Bruce-Partington Plans*
2 Dec	*The Mazarin Stone*
6 Jan	*The Missing Three-Quarter*
3 Feb	*The Copper Beeches*
3 March	*The Final Problem*

SHERLOCK HOLMES STORIES
BBC Home Service, 11 Oct–15 Nov 1957.
In Children's Hour. Written by Felix Felton.
Sherlock Holmes: Carleton Hobbs. Dr Watson: Norman Shelley.

11 Oct	*The Naval Treaty*
18 Oct	*The Five Orange Pips*
25 Oct	*The Blue Carbuncle*
1 Nov	*The Red-Headed League*
8 Nov	*The Three Students*
15 Nov	*The Final Problem*

THE HOUND OF THE BASKERVILLES
BBC Light Programme, 6 instalments, 6 Apr–11 May 1958.
Written by Felix Felton.
Sherlock Holmes: Carleton Hobbs. Dr Watson: Norman Shelley.

THE BLUE CARBUNCLE
BBC Home Service, 20 June 1958. Schools broadcasts – Senior English.
Sherlock Holmes: Carleton Hobbs.

SHERLOCK HOLMES
BBC, 15 Nov 1958.
Scenes from the stage play by William Gillette. Written and produced by Raymond Raikes.
The first stereophonic drama broadcast. 28min.
Sherlock Holmes: Hugh Manning. Dr Watson: Leigh Crutchley. Professor Robert Moriarty: Baliol Holloway.

SHERLOCK HOLMES
BBC Light Programme, 12 May–25 Aug 1959.
Written by Michael Hardwick.

12 May	*The Man with the Twisted Lip*
30 June	*The Beryl Coronet*
4 Aug	*Blanched Soldier*
11 Aug	*The Copper Beeches*
18 Aug	*The Noble Bachelor*
25 Aug	*Shoscombe Old Place*

THE SIGN OF FOUR
BBC Light Programme, 5 instalments, 16 May–13 June 1959.
Written by Felix Felton.
Sherlock Holmes: Richard Hurndall. Dr Watson: Bryan Coleman.

DE TRE STUDENTERNA (The Three Students) Sweden
Swedish Channel 1, 27 Dec 1959.
Written by Gunnar Lie.
Sherlock Holmes: Georg Årlin. Dr Watson: Ragnar Falck.

DEN GULDBÅGADE PINCENEN (The Golden Pince-Nez)
Swedish Channel 1, 3 Jan 1960.
Written by Gunnar Lie.
Sherlock Holmes: Georg Årlin. Dr Watson: Ragnar Falck.

SCRAPBOOK FOR 1910 – scene from *The Speckled Band*
BBC, 10 Feb 1960.
Sherlock Holmes: Carleton Hobbs. Dr Watson: Leslie Perrins.

SHERLOCK HOLMES
BBC Light Programme, 23 Feb–31 May 1960.
Written by Michael Hardwick.
Sherlock Holmes: Carleton Hobbs. Dr Watson: Norman Shelley. Inspector Lestrade: Humphrey Morton.

23 Feb	*The Stockbroker's Clerk*
22 March	*The Naval Treaty*
5 Apr	*The Greek Interpreter*
19 Apr	*The Cardboard Box*
3 May	*Lady Frances Carfax*
17 May	*The Engineer's Thumb*
31 May	*The Illustrious Client*

THE VALLEY OF FEAR
BBC Home Service, 31 Dec 1960.
In the series Saturday Night Theatre. Repeated 2 Jan 1961, 3 Feb and 5 Feb 1968.

Written by Michael Hardwick.
Sherlock Holmes: Carleton Hobbs. Dr Watson: Norman Shelley.

THE HOUND OF THE BASKERVILLES
BBC Home Service, 5 Aug 1961. Repeated 11 Apr 1965.
Written by Felix Felton.
Sherlock Holmes: Carleton Hobbs. Dr Watson: Nigel Bruce.

SHERLOCK HOLMES
BBC Light Programme, 27 Nov 1961–8 Jan 1962. 6 broadcasts.
Written by Michael Hardwick.
Sherlock Holmes: Carleton Hobbs. Dr Watson: Norman Shelley.

27 Nov	*The Empty House*
4 Dec	*The Reigate Squires*
11 Dec	*The Resident Patient*
18 Dec	*Charles Augustus Milverton*
1 Jan	*Thor Bridge*
8 Jan	*The Priory School*

SHERLOCK HOLMES
BBC Light Programme, 17 July–4 Sept 1962. 8 broadcasts.
Written by Michael Hardwick.
Sherlock Holmes: Carleton Hobbs. Dr Watson: Norman Shelley.

17 July	*The Speckled Band*
24 July	*Silver Blaze*
31 July	*The Musgrave Ritual*
7 Aug	*The Golden Pince-Nez*
14 Aug	*The Missing Three-Quarter*
21 Aug	*Abbey Grange*
28 Aug	*The Devil's Foot*
4 Sept	*The Mazarin Stone*

A STUDY IN SCARLET
BBC Home Service, 22 Dec 1962.
Written by Michael Hardwick.
Sherlock Holmes: Carleton Hobbs. Dr Watson: Norman Shelley.

THE SIGN OF FOUR
BBC Home Service, 2 March 1963.
Written by Michael Hardwick.
Sherlock Holmes: Carleton Hobbs. Dr Watson: Norman Shelley.

SHERLOCK HOLMES RETURNS
BBC Light Programme, 7 Aug–9 Oct 1964. 10 broadcasts.
Written by Michael Hardwick.
Sherlock Holmes: Carleton Hobbs. Dr Watson: Norman Shelley. Inspector Lestrade: Humphrey Morton.

7 Aug	*Abbey Grange**
14 Aug	*The Mazarin Stone**
21 Aug	*The Solitary Cyclist*
28 Aug	*The Bruce-Partington Plans*
4 Sept	*The Three Garridebs*
11 Sept	*The Norwood Builder*
18 Sept	*The Sussex Vampire*
25 Sept	*The Red-Headed League*
2 Oct	*The Three Gables*
9 Oct	*The Retired Colourman*

* Repeated from the 1962 *Sherlock Holmes* series.

THE MAN WHO WAS SHERLOCK HOLMES
BBC, 16 Dec 1964.
'An investigation into the relationship between the famous detective and his creator.' Written by Michael and Mollie Hardwick.

SHERLOCK HOLMES AGAIN
BBC Light Programme, 21 Nov 1966–16 Jan 1967. 9 broadcasts.
Written by Michael Hardwick.
Sherlock Holmes: Carleton Hobbs. Dr Watson: Norman Shelley.

21 Nov	*A Scandal in Bohemia*
28 Nov	*The Five Orange Pips*
5 Dec	*The Six Napoleons*
12 Dec	*The Boscombe Valley Mystery*
19 Dec	*The Crooked Man*
26 Dec	*Wisteria Lodge*
2 Jan	*The Dying Detective*
9 Jan	*The Second Stain*
16 Jan	*The Final Problem*

(SHERLOCK HOLMES)   Switzerland
Geneva-Lausanne. Radio Suisse Romande, 22 May 1967–(?) 6 broadcasts.
Sherlock Holmes: Marcel Imhoff.

22 May	*L'Ecole du Prieure* (The Priory School)
21 Aug	*Le Traité Naval* (The Naval Treaty)
(?)	*Le Tordu* (The Man with the Twisted Lip)

(?)	*Peter le Noir* (Black Peter)
(?)	*L'Escarboucle Bleu* (The Blue Carbuncle)
(?)	*Le Mystère du Val Boscombe* (The Boscombe Valley Mystery)

MÄSTERDETEKIVER OCH ANDRA SKÄRPTA (Master Detectives and other Smart People)   Sweden
Swedish Channel 1, 26 and 28 Sept 1967.
Sherlock Holmes: Stig Ericsson.

26 Sept	Scene from *The Sign of Four*
28 Sept	*Dr Watson's Watch* (from *The Sign of Four*)

SHERLOCK HOLMES
BBC Radio 2, 24 June–10 July 1969. 6 broadcasts.
Written by Michael Hardwick.
Sherlock Holmes: Carleton Hobbs. Dr Watson: Norman Shelley.

24 June	*The Dancing Man*
26 June	*A Case of Identity*
1 July	*Black Peter*
3 July	*The Red Circle*
8 July	*The Lion's Mane*
10 July	*His Last Bow*

BASKERVILLES HUND (The Hound of the Baskervilles)   Sweden
Swedish Channel 1, 5 instalments, 9 Jan–6 Feb 1971. Repeated 2 Dec–30 Dec 1972, and 4 Dec 1972–1 Jan 1973.
Sherlock Holmes: Georg Årlin. Dr Watson: Gösta Prüzelius.

(SHERLOCK HOLMES)   Sweden
Swedish Channel 3, 17 Feb–10 March 1974. 4 broadcasts.
Written by Eva Paske and Ittla Frodi.
Sherlock Holmes: Jan Blomberg. Dr Watson: Gösta Prüzelius.

17 Feb	*Mazarinstenen* (The Mazarin Stone)
24 Feb	*Den Bla Karbunkeln* (The Blue Carbuncle)
3 March	*Flottfördraget* (The Naval Treaty)
10 March	*De Rödhårigas Förening* (The Red-Headed League)

Sherlock Holmes on Television

This list covers television plays only. Films made for television are in the section 'Sherlock Holmes on Film'.

THE THREE GARRIDEBS
Sherlock Holmes: Louis Hector   New York Television   1937

THE MAZARIN STONE   BBC Television   29 July 1951
Sherlock Holmes: Andrew Osborn. Dr Watson: Philip King.

FIRST BBC TELEVISION SERIES, 1951

Adapted: C. A. Lejeune.
Sherlock Holmes: Alan Wheatley. Dr Watson: Raymond Francis. Inspector Lestrade: Bill Owen.

20 Oct 1951	*The Empty House*
27 Oct 1951	*A Scandal in Bohemia*
3 Nov 1951	*The Dying Detective*
17 Nov 1951	*The Reigate Squires*
24 Nov 1951	*The Red-Headed League*
1 Dec 1951	*The Second Stain*

THE BLACK BARONET   CBS Television USA   26 May 1953
Based on the story by Adrian Conan Doyle and transmitted by CBS in their *Suspense* series.
Sherlock Holmes: Basil Rathbone. Dr Watson: Martyn Green.

THE SPECKLED BAND   BBC Television   18 May 1964
Transmitted in the series *Detective*. Repeated 25 Sept 1964. The pilot programme for the ensuing series.
Sherlock Holmes: Douglas Wilmer. Dr Watson: Nigel Stock.

SECOND BBC TELEVISION SERIES, 1965

Prod: David Goddard. Sherlock Holmes: Douglas Wilmer. Dr Watson: Nigel Stock.

20 Feb 1965	
Repeated 15 Nov 1966	*The Illustrious Client*
27 Feb 1965	
Repeated 8 Aug 1966	*The Devil's Foot*
6 March 1965	
Repeated 15 Aug 1966	*The Copper Beeches*
13 March 1965	
Repeated 5 Sept 1966	*The Red-Headed League*
20 March 1965	
Repeated 29 Aug 1966	*The Abbey Grange*
27 March 1965	
Repeated 22 Aug 1966	*The Six Napoleons*
3 Apr 1965	
Repeated 12 Sept 1966	*The Man with the Twisted Lip*
10 Apr 1965	
Repeated 19 Sept 1966	*The Beryl Coronet*
17 Apr 1965	
Repeated 26 Sept 1966	*The Bruce-Partington Plans*
24 Apr 1965	
Repeated 3 Oct 1966	*Charles Augustus Milverton*
1 May 1965	
Repeated 21 Oct 1966	*The Retired Colourman*
8 May 1965	
Repeated 28 Oct 1966	*The Disappearance of Lady Frances Carfax*

THIRD BBC TELEVISION SERIES, 1968

Prod: William Sterling. Sherlock Holmes: Peter Cushing. Dr Watson: Nigel Stock.

9 Sept 1968	*The Second Stain*
16 Sept 1968	*A Study in Scarlet*
23 Sept 1968	*The Dancing Men*
30 Sept 1968–	
7 Oct 1968	*The Hound of the Baskervilles* (Parts 1 and 2)
14 Oct 1968	*The Boscombe Valley Mystery*
21 Oct 1968	*The Greek Interpreter*
28 Oct 1968	*The Naval Treaty*
4 Nov 1968	*Thor Bridge*
11 Nov 1968	*The Musgrave Ritual*
18 Nov 1968	*Black Peter*

25 Nov 1968	*Wisteria Lodge*
2 Dec 1968	*Shoscombe Old Place*
9 Dec 1968	*The Solitary Cyclist*
16 Dec 1968	*The Sign of Four*
23 Dec 1968	*The Blue Carbuncle*

ELEMENTARY MY DEAR WATSON   BBC Television   18 Jan 1973
Written by N. F. Simpson. In the series *Comedy Playhouse*.
Sherlock Holmes: John Cleese. Dr Watson: William Rushton.
An authorised spoof, intended as the pilot for a series which fortunately seems
to have been abandoned.

DR WATSON AND THE DARKWATER HALL MYSTERY
BBC Television   Christmas 1974
Written by Kingsley Amis.
Dr Watson: Edward Fox.
A mystery dealt with by Watson, without the appearance of Holmes at all.

Sherlock Holmes on Records

A brief recording of a sequence from his play was made by William Gillette at a private party in 1936. It was issued in the USA as *Sherlock Holmes Explained by His Creator Sir Arthur Conan Doyle and Presented in Action by William Gillette* by National Vocarium on TNV-109, in 1939 and on the Gotham LP *History Speaks* in 1961.

Two of the Harry Alan Towers 1954 broadcasts (see p 184) were issued in Great Britain by Decca on one LP, LK 4164. The programmes were *Dr Watson Meets Sherlock Holmes* (which was partly from *A Study in Scarlet* and partly from *Charles Augustus Milverton*) and *The Final Problem*.

Basil Rathbone recorded a series of readings from five of the stories for Audio Book Company Records in the USA, on AB 5053 to AB 5060.

The Blue Carbuncle	
The Final Problem	
The Red-Headed League	1958
A Scandal in Bohemia	
The Speckled Band	

Basil Rathbone recorded a further series of readings for Caedmon in 1962–3.

The Speckled Band	TC 1172	1963
The Final Problem		
The Red-Headed League	TC 1208	1966
A Scandal in Bohemia	TC 1220	1967
Silver Blaze	TC 1240	1967

To correspond with the opening of the musical *Baker Street*, MGM issued an LP of the principal songs on E 7000 OC (SE 7000 C stereo), with the original cast. 1965.

Conquest Children's Records   EP No CE 1048, c 1965
The Speckled Band. Written by Morys Aberdare and Fiona Bentley.
Sherlock Holmes: John Clements. Dr Watson: Walter Fitzgerald.

Michael and Mollie Hardwick wrote and produced a series of dramatisations specifically for gramophone records, which were made by Discourses Ltd in 1970.
Sherlock Holmes: Robert Hardy. Dr Watson: Nigel Stock.

The Speckled Band *The Blue Carbuncle*	} DCO 1210
Charles Augustus Milverton *Black Peter*	} DCO 1211
The Norwood Builder *Lady Frances Carfax*	} DCO 1212
Shoscombe Old Place *The Illustrious Client*	} DCO 1213

NBC radio broadcast of 6 Nov 1939, on Radiola LP No 5, 1971.
The Bruce-Partington Plans from *The Adventures of Sherlock Holmes* (see pp 173–4).
Sherlock Holmes: Basil Rathbone. Dr Watson: Nigel Bruce.

CBS radio broadcast of 25 Sept 1938, on Radiola   LP No MR–1036, 1974
William Gillette's play *Sherlock Holmes* (see p 173).
Sherlock Holmes: Orson Welles. Dr Watson: Ray Collins.

Index